ADVENTURIST
LIVING

How to unlock adventure in your everyday life

FELICIA LEIJA

Dedicated to Allen "Doc" McCray.

I am the adventurist living woman

I am today because of you.

CONTENTS

Introduction 1

There is Something "More" 5

Preparing for your adventure 20

The Treasure Map 44

Your Whole Life Adventure: The Life Wheel 56

It begins with a dream. 72

Goals: The "X" on Your Treasure Map 85

Adventure Roadblocks: Limiting Beliefs 114

The Adventure Zone: Decision Making 176

Creating Your Adventure Story 194

Design Your Days: Developing Routines 204

GO Live YOUR Adventure 221

INTRODUCTION

―――――――●◆●―――――――

"Inside us all is an adventure."

– Author Unknown

―――――――●●●●●●―――――――

I had always been drawn to the word adventure, long before I was living the life. I am captivated by words. I am quick to research their definitions and all of their synonyms. Certain words grab my attention immediately, like a jolt of espresso, while others have more of a gentle drawing about them that grows over time. All of that to say, I give great attention to the words that I am gravitating toward, like a moth to a flame. I have realized that these words are significant to where I am in my life, where I want to go in my life, and who I want to become in my life. Some words are for a period of time, to either make sense of the season I am in or the focus of what I want that season to be and accomplish. And then there are the words that I believe are the banners

1

over our life. Essentially, what you might consider the *motto* of our lives. Adventure has become by banner word – the slogan of my life. But not in the typical sense or definition of the word.

What triggered this book was a response. Over the past five or so years, I had been getting social media messages and also hearing it from friends, acquaintances, and colleagues, "You are goals" or "I wish I had the life you have" or "you're such an adventurer." I would get these messages in response to the many places I travel to, the things I try and explore, and the training I get to do worldwide. Also, I was able to work remotely, and even in making a move to live in Puerto Rico and embrace that incredible Caribbean life.

At first (and it still is), it was all so crazy. I now have a life that people desire? This girl that came from nothing, a broken home, being kicked out of school when she was 15 years old (and working ever since), was a hider and a runner, having no ambitions or dreams, being completely stuck most of her life, now has a life that others are inspired by? It is so absolutely humbling, and can I just say, so crazy cool at the same time!

When I initially began receiving these messages, I knew I didn't want just to say, "thank you, I am blessed!" or the easy reply of "you can live this life too" (although I genuinely believe all of us can). Something inside me knew I had a more important message to convey. The need, the charge, to express that, yes, being able to travel all over the world, speak, train, continue to explore and try new things and live on a beautiful island is all so very incredible and fantastic. I am grateful for every experience, but I wanted to let everyone know that every single day is magical, regardless if I was on a beautiful Caribbean island or in my 2-bedroom condo in the desert of Phoenix, AZ. I felt it necessary to share that yes, travel and exploring are incredible gifts, but the magic of life is in every day of life. That we have within us the ability to experience adventure every single day of our lives.

That book is meant to spark the calling within you, to awaken that adventure in you, to the reality, you can genuinely live every day. And since I have done it and am doing it, I know anyone can.

THERE IS SOMETHING "MORE"

"I feel like there is something more."

That phrase was the constant aching, gnawing, almost tormenting whisper calling from deep within me for over a decade.

I often wondered if I was destined to live the life I was living. That this was the lot I had been given and that the call for more inside was something to be silenced. Maybe that's just the way life is. I didn't know of anyone personally who I could say, "they are living life, and I want to be like them." I had tried to convince myself the idea of "there is something more" was a fairytale, something only seen and experienced in movies or those that had a different background than me or just better luck than I did. The story I was telling myself to get through life (and others had told me as well) was just to be grateful for what you have and don't hope for too much more.

But the aching whisper of more within my heart and soul never subsided. It only grew louder. I had a decade of journals to prove it. I wrote too many times to count, "I feel like there is something more God." Let's say I did believe that something more was indeed accessible to me. Then came the painful fact that I had absolutely no clue how to get it, find it, unlock it, discover it. How does one move into the more of life? I didn't even know what that would look like. The people around me and who I had access to at the time weren't displaying this something more in their own lives. I kept going around in this small, small circle in my mind, and I felt stuck. Being honest, I had felt stuck my entire life.

The trap of good. Living a good life.

I had a good job. I was in good health. Compared to most of the world, compared to where I had come from (I didn't choose the thug life, the thug life chose me – I had to), I had a good life, I had a roof over my head, and clothes on my back.

I had a decent and pretty good job, despite my past and lack of formal education, any other GED – Good Enough Diploma - people out there? I had good friends. I should be grateful, right? And I was.

But the aching whisper of more within
my heart and soul never subsided.
It only grew louder.

—————————•••●●••—————————

I had fallen into the trap that good was well, good, when in fact, it is the enemy of great. Good will keep you stuck. Good will keep you comfortable. Good will keep you from ever stepping out and experiencing life fully. Good will keep you from experiencing the more that calls out to you.

How many of us have settled for or are currently settling for the "good" and never ventured into the great that is continuously calling out to us? Why is it calling? It continues to call because it is in our very make-up. Get that. Reread it. It is in our DNA, deposited from the Creator of the Universe, to experience the more that comes from truly living.

We can get the state of being grateful and content mixed up with the idea that we shouldn't aspire for more. Somehow, somewhere, the world has gotten it twisted. The truth is we are created for greatness. We are made in the image of God. You are created for greatness, and you are created in the image of God.

The powerful poem by Maryanne Williamson has a beautiful way of expressing this:

"Our greatest fear is not that we are inadequate. Our deepest fear is that we are powerful beyond measure. It is our light, not our darkness that that most frightens us. We ask ourselves, who am I to be brilliant, gorgeous, talented, fabulous? Actually, who are you not to be? Your playing small does not serve the world. We were born to make manifest the glory of God that is within us. And as we let our own light shine, we unconsciously give other people permission to do the same."

You were born to shine.

Statistics, research, and people's stories reveal that most people live a fraction of their full potential. Their dreams remain dormant, unfulfilled, and filed away in the overly used "I wish _____" folder of their heart.

Why a lot of dreams and goals end up in the "I wish ____" or the "one day I will ____" folders can be attributed to one of the greatest tragedies of this life (and you only get one): and that is going through life on automatic pilot and remaining in status quo. It's like living Groundhog's Day every day. Your autopilot days become autopilot weeks, weeks make up months, months make up years, and then comes the one day we wake up, decades have passed by, and we are nearing the end of their lives and pulling out all those deposits into the "I wish" folder, which now have become regrets.

For others, something tragic suddenly happens, or they receive a bad health report, and it is at that moment they are faced with the blaring reality of how they have spent their life. It is here they wish they would have made the most of their time and think about all the ways they would have done things differently.

I can speak to that because that was me. I was living every day in automatic pilot, waiting for something magical to happen in my life. I was waiting for life to happen to me instead of making life happen for me. I was secretly hoping something external would happen to rescue me from my world. What I hadn't realized was that all the while, the magic was internal; it was inside me.

> *I was waiting for life*
> *to happen to me,*
> *instead of making life*
> *happen for me.*

──────────•••●●••──────────

I had to step out of the wanting to be rescued mentality, thinking that someone else, something else, or chance was the answer. I had to take responsibility for my own life, my own growth.

What is interesting is that most of the people around me at the time perceived my life to be very intriguing and free. I was known as that fascinating, gypsy, hippie soul. Why would they think that way? Oh, that's because I would easily just up and quit a job at the drop of a hat and travel to a distant country. I wore natural and free-flowing clothing and jewelry (so much so I opened up a boutique called The Happy Hippie). I was regularly called a free spirit, and I am not going to lie, I enjoyed that title. I enjoyed how people viewed me, even though it felt like a lie when I got real with myself. That is because it was coming from the wrong place. I wasn't running to life; I was running from life. Until...

As mentioned before, if you were to take a look at my journals (I highly recommend journaling if you do not already) during the decade before the shifting moment in my life, you would find pages filled with the following: "I feel like there is something more" and "I need to go!". That was my runner side speaking and more about that in a later chapter, but those were proclamations of my heart and soul desperately seeking after more.

I don't despise that decade. I am thankful for it. I am beyond grateful that God would not allow that whisper (a very loud whisper) ever to go away or even diminish. I don't believe he just let it continue, I think he was the one doing the calling. The fact that God loves us, his kiddos, so much he never stops calling us to more, is so incredibly mind-blowing in itself.

It doesn't mean it didn't hurt, though. One thing about searching is that when you find what you're looking for, you know it.

The day that forever changed my life.

I was invited by two close friends to attend an all-day (deep sigh, doesn't sound fun) workshop by Dr. Allen McCray of Life Impact LLC on the DISC personality styles. My friends had attended his workshops before and had been bugging me to attend, that they were life-changing, and I would not regret going.

Oh yeah, I was skeptical. I also didn't like the idea of my whole day being at a seminar. But I trusted these friends and figured worst-case scenario, I will work on different things while in the class, and if I get bored or I can always just leave.

Little did I know that for an entire eight hours, I would be locked in! I created and found places to take notes since I had filled the six-page handout (both sides) with notes and ah-ha moments I was experiencing! At the end of the eight-hours, I didn't want it to end. I wanted more! Something was beginning to be awakened, and that something was me. I felt exhilarated and more alive than ever when I left. Then I went home after the workshop and was doing the dishes before I was due to meet up with my sister a little later that evening, and that's when it happened.

I lost it. I literally LOST IT.

Yes, I had a breakdown. Well, what I would translate to being a breakdown. It happened right there at my kitchen sink. It consisted of me crying uncontrollably (you know that ugly cry, distorted face, body convulsing, snot everywhere). The thoughts to myself during all of this were, "I am going to have to be institutionalized!", "I can't keep it together!", "I'm losing it!". I pictured myself being put in a straitjacket and being committed. I know, a bit extreme and entertaining (well now), but that is what it felt like. Ever been there?

Well, I hadn't.

Until that moment, I had been emotionally locked up, walled up, for my entire life, but I consciously hadn't realized that. My self-perception was that I was tough. I prided myself on my ability to keep it together. In all honesty, I had intolerance or lack of compassion for those that were emotionally up and down, or what I would have considered emotionally unstable. Part of that was due to the household I grew up in – my parents were always arguing and physically fighting. I had been in a protective mode since I was a child, without knowing. I had emotionally put walls up to survive and cope.

Those walls had stayed sturdy and intact well up into my adulthood. And now, at the kitchen sink, those walls had begun breaking down, and it scared the hell out of me!

I immediately reached out to Dr. Allen McCray for help, the one who had done the workshop, this workshop that I blamed solely for this breakdown. My email (while still sobbing) to him said something like this: "I loved your workshop, but I am jacked up! I need a session with you!".

I had never reached out for counseling before (that wasn't court-ordered by a judge, your girl has a past), but I knew I needed help, and I believed he was the one who could help me.

Side note, to begin living an adventurist life, it will be necessary for you to do things you have never done before.

Early that following week, I had my first session, and it changed my life. It changed the entire direction of my life. I will get into the details of our session in a later chapter, but what happened during the workshop was that memories and incidents from my childhood began to be unearthed because the seminar's material had awakened my self-awareness. Things were brought to light that had been holding back since I was eight years old. Yes, eight years old! The tools I received for healing and moving forward that day changed the entire direction of my life. I also learned that you can't just lock up one emotion. You're either emotionally open, or you are closed. You experience all of them or none of them entirely. What I was experiencing was an eruption of emotion that had been stuffed down and locked up for decades. It was so scary, but it was exhilarating at the same time. I was alive!

> *To begin living an adventurist life,*
> *it will be necessary for you to do things*
> *you have never done before.*

——————————•◦●◦•——————————

What happened during that session was incredible. But what was equally incredible, if not more, was that in that session, I knew I was encountering who had the answers to the more I had been searching for. I wanted what Dr. McCray had, and I wanted to learn from him. I wanted to do what he did. And I was determined to get it.

For the first time in my life, I got serious with the prayers, decisions, and actions for my own life. Until that moment, I had always been there for others, praying hard for others, believing for others, essentially living through others. Now, it was time I got bold in the prayers for myself. My first bold item? Dr. McCray had an internship, and I was going to be in it. Watch me.

The visual I can give of what had happened inside me and what I continue to use to this day when making a significant decision in my life and commitment is that I had drawn a line in the sand. I was moving forward. I was not going to stay in the same place. If I were to fall, it would be falling forward, not backward.

I didn't realize it at the moment, but what I had done was set a goal. Until then, I had never been the goal-setting type or even dreaming type. This is because I didn't know who I was, what I was interested in, what my passions were because I had been locked up for so long, and I also feared disappointment. But now, I had a clear vision of where I wanted to go and had an aim. I was going into unchartered territory, new territory, unknown territory. I had never even dreamed of being in someone's internship. What's an internship?!

That is what adventurist living is. It is about experiencing unknown and new territory in our lives, which is growth. We can encounter adventurist living in every area of our lives.

I won't give it all away at once, but I got way more than I ever dreamed of. I didn't just get into Dr. McCray's internship; I began working with him, partnering with him in his business, learning from him firsthand, doing and experiencing life with him and his beautiful bride Sharon. When I accepted the position to work with him, he told me this: "working with me, things will be more caught than taught," and he was so right.

That goal, of being in his internship, was my goal, which became a big ole red "X" on my adventurist living treasure map, my personal growth map. I will get more into the treasure map in a later chapter.

I wanted to share my story with you, those that feel stuck, those that feel like there is something more, those that are unsure how to get it. I know what that feels like, and I believe it is no mistake you are reading this book right now. I know that if I can discover and unlock the more in my life, live out my potential and live the life I was created to, so can you. I believe 100% that you can! But, more importantly, I hope that during your journey through this book, you begin to believe you can.

I am so glad you are here. I am giddy! I am excited! I hope you are too!

Let the adventure begin!

PREPARING FOR YOUR ADVENTURE

---◆---

"The road is there, it will always be there. You just have to decide to take it."

- Chris Humphrey

---●---

With any trip, it's essential to pack, right? You prepare for where you are going and what you will be doing. As with any trip, you try to go in as prepared as you can, and the rest comes from the experience of what you encounter in the journey – that is adventurist living.

Living a life of adventure is a mindset, and since this book is all about adventurist living, I will keep mentioning it! That way you can begin thinking of your entire life as an adventure. As you step into new and unknown terrain and feel the uncomfortableness that accompanies those steps, you will be able to shift your mind and awareness and say to yourself, "Oh yeah, this is an adventure, my adventure, that's why I am uncomfortable, this is new!"

In preparation, picture yourself having a backpack, and you are going to put some tools in it for you to carry with you to pull from when needed. Revisit and pull out these tools as much as you need to until they become a part of you and habitual response.

Okay, let's pack!

1.COMMITMENT.

The first thing to bring on your journey is your commitment. In simple terms, commitment means to make a promise. Commitment means making a promise to yourself and to something. When it comes to adventurist living, that means making a promise to yourself to grow and experience those unknown and new territories that come with you going beyond anywhere you have been before in life. You are making a promise to yourself to deeply experience this life.

No one can commit for you, just as no one can take your journey for you. It is up to you. If you're leery of commitment due to broken promises and commitments to yourself in the past, that's okay, we all have them.

This is a new day though, and if you're alive and breathing, this is your opportunity to reset, draw your line in the sand, and decide you are moving forward (and remember, at times even falling forward, because it will happen) in mindset, action, and heart to live your life to the fullest, every single day.

2. AN OPEN MIND.

An open mind is crucial. We can have one of two mindsets we are operating in: an open-mindset (also known as a growth mindset) or a closed mindset (a fixed mindset).

In order to grow at all, and in any area of our lives, an open mind is necessary. The following is an illustration that I do at the beginning of our self-leadership workshops to help participants become more open-minded.

I am going to ask you what I ask those attending the workshops: "by a raise of hands, who here considers themselves to be pretty open-minded?". Yes, you do it too. If you consider yourself to be open-minded, raise that hand!

Now, let's do a little exercise to see just how open-minded you are.

Take a look at the illustration below:

How many squares do you see?

Take your time, this isn't a race. How many squares do you see? Decide your answer before you continue reading. Yes, STOP reading (oooooh, you're sneaky) and do the exercise before reading the answer. If you'd like to, you can visit my website right now by going here: https://adventuristliving.com/bookresources and watch a video illustration of this exercise.

After looking at the squares above or watching the video, what number did you come up with? I can tell you that the most common numbers I get when in a workshop are 16, 17, 21, 24...

But what if I told you that there are *at least* 46 squares in this illustration? You may think that's crazy, but it's true. Let's see how:

1-16 squares: outlined in black

17: the overall square

18 - 26: 4x4 squares

27- 30: 3x3 squares

31- 46: solid squares (illustrated with the green).

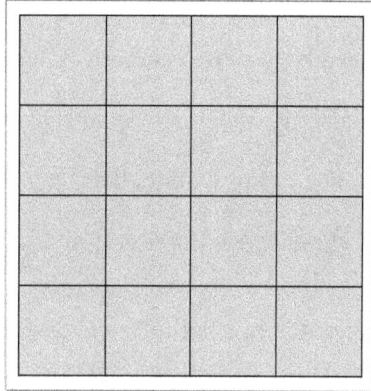

Squares 31-46 is where most people get stuck.

There are actually 16 additional squares. If you're having a problem seeing them, hopefully this will help:

1 square is outlined in black, example:

But then there is a whole other square that is solid and NOT

outlined:

How many of you saw those? Be honest! I know I didn't the first time I was exposed to this exercise!

What this illustration represents is how many times when faced with new situations, tough conversations, setting new goals, dreaming, challenges, opportunities, maybe reading a book and applying it, that we only see 16, 17, 21, 24 squares, or should I say possibilities?

What we can fail to see is that there is so much more to be seen, which comes with a new level of open-mindedness you can experience!

I had stated that there is a minimum of 46 squares. This is because our 46 square answer was challenged once during one of our workshops. When doing this illustration, a mathematician raised his hand and said he could see hundreds of squares! That is because he could see the 3-D possibilities. Which was a great reminder to us doing the workshop that there is always a new level of growth and open-mindedness to go to... that's exciting!

Let's go a little further because I want you to get this open-mindedness thing because it's crucial.

Remember, you can visit
https://adventuristliving.com/bookresources to see a video
illustration of the square exercise.

Here is another illustration of what a difference it makes in
our lives between having a closed-mindset (fixed mindset)
and an open-mindset (growth mindset).

Take a look at the funnel below:

CLOSED MIND-SET

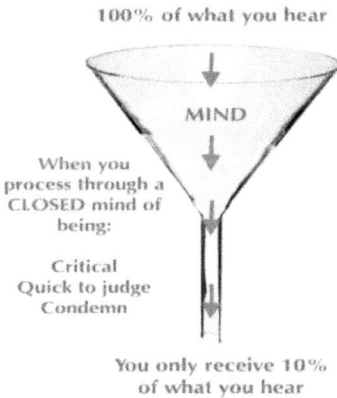

100% of what you hear

MIND

When you
process through a
CLOSED mind of
being:

Critical
Quick to judge
Condemn

You only receive 10%
of what you hear

When we hear, watch, read, with a closed mind, which means
we are quick to judge something, quick to condemn it, shoot
it down, be critical, remain fixed in our thinking, as the funnel

illustrates, we only (at best) can receive 10% of what was put before us.

Not ideal for growth, right? Who wants only to receive 10% of what they are hearing and seeing, and that's at best? Especially if you're going to experience life at a different level, which guess what, requires growth. What's incredible is that at any moment, you can decide to pursue being more open-minded (and we all can become more open-minded) and have the capability to flip that funnel, begin cultivating a growth mindset. And then this is what happens...

OPEN MINDSET

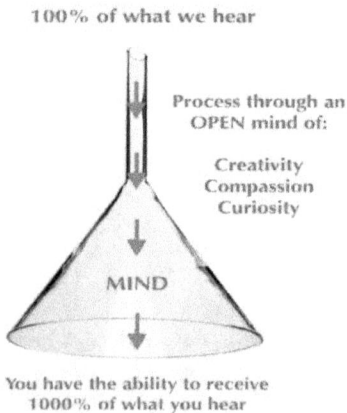

100% of what we hear

Process through an OPEN mind of:

Creativity
Compassion
Curiosity

MIND

You have the ability to receive 1000% of what you hear

When you shift to becoming more open-minded, this is where the magic begins happening. When you have an open mind, which means processing what you are hearing, seeing, and experiencing with creativity, compassion, with curiosity, you can receive a 1000% of what is put before you! Yes, you read that right, one-THOUSAND percent. That is because you have now engaged your imagination. Ideas start coming, and you can expand further than the actual presented information and experience itself.

Now, if that's not cool and exciting, I am not sure what is!

You can now begin to catch yourself and be aware when you're operating in a closed mindset and make the shift to being more open-minded. This requires being present and practicing self-awareness. Here are the descriptors of a closed mindset and an open mindset to help you identify which attitude you are operating in:

Closed Mind: Judgmental of self and others, fears making a mistake/failing, critical, shoots down new ideas, lives in a pattern of negativity, blames others for failure (victim mentality).

Open Mind: Curious with self and others, compassionate with self and others, learns from mistakes, grows forward, recognizes negative patterns, takes steps to correct, takes responsibility for failures, and makes preparations for the next opportunity.

Begin asking yourself questions like: "how would it be for me to be curious in this situation or ask what I am hearing?" "How could I get the MOST out of what I am experiencing right now?" "I know I have had a fixed opinion on this subject before, but what would it look like to be flexible and open-minded?" "What growth opportunities are before me right now?"

Can you begin feeling the difference within yourself with these questions?

We all can continue to grow in this area. Like being compassionate and curious with what you are experiencing, also practice being compassionate and curious with yourself throughout this whole book, through this process, and in life.

As with the square illustration, you can go to https://adventuristliving.com/bookresources to see the funnel example on video.

3.COMPASSION AND CURIOSITY.

Since we just talked about compassion and curiosity, it's a perfect opportunity to introduce it as an essential item for bringing along on the trip of life.

As humans, we tend to lean towards beating up and being tough on ourselves on the regular. If beating ourselves up worked, well, we'd all be the most successful human beings on the planet! But guess what. It doesn't.

Just as with catching ourselves in our moments of fixed mindsets, you want to apply that same principle of catching yourself when you are being critical of yourself, condemning yourself, or judging yourself.

To truly live an adventurist life and deeply experience this journey, it's necessary to be kind with yourself, just as you would with a dear friend. The key is to practice self-awareness and to catch yourself (because you can't change anything you're not aware of – we will cover that later) when you're in that place. Catching yourself in the act is a lifelong process, and it's a continual work. And it's worth it.

If you're someone that tends to beat yourself up (and we've all been there, it's built into our human nature), then you probably have made comments to yourself that sound somewhat like the following: "I shouldn't have done that," "I should've done that.", "I can't believe I did that," "So stupid." "Why don't I ever learn.", "I'm so frustrated with myself.", "I can't get anything right.". That's just a few I have commonly heard and have personally used on myself in the past.

> *It's necessary to be kind with yourself,*
> *as you would be with a dear friend.*

————————•••●●••————————

When making the switch to being compassionate and curious, the questions you can ask yourself are: "How would it look to extend compassion to myself in this situation?" "How would

I speak to a dear friend if they were experiencing this?" "If I were to get curious about why I am thinking this way, where would I say it's coming from?" And any other questions you may come up with.

Can you feel the difference? How would this change your life if you began practicing compassion and curiosity like this in your life? It's powerful, right? Practicing this alone can be a game-changer.

Remember, adventurist living is an *inside* job first, which then begins expressing itself outwardly. Practice being compassionate and curious with yourself and experience the internal difference with yourself. Remember, treat *yourself* like a dear friend.

4.TAKE ACTION.

If I were to sum up personal development in four practices, it would be: to get tools from those that have been successful in where you want to go, embrace that it is a process and not an event (no overnight successes), obtain the mindset needed to become who you were created to be and go to new levels of living and put into action the tools you have received.

Tools, process, mindset, and action.

Everything else falls under one of those topics. In this book, you will receive several different tools. If you put them into practice, you will experience a life full of adventure, growth and count yourself amongst those who are profoundly experiencing life every day.

These are the same tools I have practiced and continue to practice in my daily life that unlocked the more that had always been within me and the reality of living an adventurist life. These tools are ones I have learned from mentors, coaches, books, courses, and personal experience.

This book will take you through a process. All of life is a process, a journey. It's more important who you become in the process than actually arriving at the destination itself.

Every day can be magical, extraordinary, full of life if you choose it and put the tools to work. Like a screwdriver or hammer, you can have the tools, but if you never use them, they accomplish nothing. So, put the tools to work.

5. CELEBRATE.

When taking action, every step and effort, no matter how small or large you feel it may be, is worth celebrating, and you want to celebrate. Research has shown that one critical step to behavior change (and our behaviors are played out in our decisions, actions, and habits) is to celebrate each small win so that your brain associates it with positive feelings. Decide something you will do, an actual physical or audible expression of the successes you experience. Do you watch football? If you do or have even seen when a player makes a touchdown, each has their way of celebrating the win they just experienced. That touchdown might have been a game-winning touchdown or a successful play. The player recognizes that it all is towards winning the overall game, and each gain is well worth celebrating.

I incorporate a few celebratory actions of my own. One is I put my hands up in the air and pull down to my sides with a GREAT BIG "YES"! Another is a mantra. I say out loud, "you're doing this, Felicia!" sometimes, I get up and do a happy dance! As you begin implementing your expressions to celebrate, take that moment to be present and experience it!

Let's go further with ways to solidify your wins because this practice can make the difference between you slowing down or even halting in your progress to not only continuing in your adventure but adding that fuel to your fire that accelerates your pace.

Share your wins with people you love.

Have your list of people that you trust and know are rooting for you. When you take a step, accomplish a win (no matter how small or big), share it with them. Something is validating and affirming when you share your successes with those that support you fully.

Take a gratitude pause.

Gratitude is very powerful. Did you know that you cannot experience gratitude and anxiety at the same time? One emotion supersedes the other. Gratitude alone you want to make not just a part of your wins, but a part of life. When it comes to being grateful for successes, it is about being thankful for the progress and the opportunities that are continually given to us.

Write it down.

Write down your wins and steps forward every day. This is different than celebrating in the moment, as it allows you to take an aerial view of your entire day, the big picture of all you accomplished.

Celebrate the losses, too.

Well, this one doesn't sound enjoyable. However, it can change the way you look at and experience losses. If you feel like you've experienced a loss, a failure, or a step backward, take the time to process it. Realize, along with those who have genuinely stepped out into the ring of life, that losses are not only inevitable, but it's there, when you risk failure, that you put yourself in the position to discover new things. You can choose to celebrate that you jumped in, you got in the game, and you're advancing in your journey. You can choose to extract every learning opportunity that was produced from what others may consider losses. That perspective turns any failure into a gain.

Research has shown that one critical step to behavior change
(and our behaviors are played out in our decisions,
actions, and habits)
is to celebrate each small win so that your brain
associates it with positive feelings.

———————••●●•••———————

Are you ready to begin celebrating? Celebrate daily every step and every effort, the little and big wins, and action taken because you are all that closer to your destination and learning along the way. As one of my favorite life quotes by Lao Tzu says, "A journey of a thousand miles begins with a single step." Don't be deceived. Your steps count!

You've gotten some of the essentials to pack and bring on your adventurous journey. Decide now that you will set your intentions to put action to what you're receiving and learning and watch how your life begins shifting.

At the end of each chapter, there will self-coaching questions (called Ah-ha's & Discovery), focusing on what you received from the chapter and challenges to take action.

Do the work. Do it for you. Don't treat this as a project, a "to-do list" to be checked off. Be intentional and present, squeeze everything out of it and every experience. Set aside at least 10-15 minutes each day, you choose, in the morning or night. Sit with yourself. Get real with yourself.

Don't feel in a rush. Let it be your time. Create an atmosphere that's enjoyable for you.

For me, that looks like playing some soft jazz or Spanish guitar lounge music, lighting a candle, having some mood lighting, and sipping on a lovely tea latte.

None of this is an assignment or a test. There are no right or wrong answers. There is no judgment (remember to practice compassion and curiosity with yourself) if you're feeling stuck. If you begin feeling stuck or frustrated, just sit with yourself and be curious about where it's coming from. All of this is part of the transformational work.

If you need to, take a break and step away and return to it later. That's okay. It's a process. But do return.

You're packed for your trip. As with any journey, you can prepare as much you can, but embarking on your trip is where the real experience happens. After all, that's what you packed for! So, let's go!

It's now time to begin your adventurist living journey.

Ah-ha's and Discovery

How have you approached new opportunities and change in the past?

_____

_____

_____

What did the open-mind exercise reveal to you?

_____

_____

_____

How is practicing compassion and curiosity with yourself going to impact your life?

_____

_____

_____

What steps are you going to take to be intentional about taking action?

_____

_____

_____

And... ACTION!

Think about an experience or situation where you know you were closed-minded. How would it have changed your experience if you had been open-minded?

_____

_____

_____

Think about something you were hard on yourself about recently. How would it be to extend compassion & curiosity with yourself? Say what you would say to yourself below as if you were talking to a good friend.

_____

_____

_____

What are you going to do to celebrate? What will your mantra(s) and physical action(s) be?

_____

_____

_____

THE TREASURE MAP

"Yes, any plunge into the unknown is reckless – but that's where the treasure lies."

Brendon Burchard, High Performance Habits

There is no magic pill, not one single event, no DeLorean (like from Back to the Future) that will poof, bring you automatically to where you want to be, or microwave you into your destination.

Transformation, growth, adventurist living, it's all a *process*.

The more we can embrace the process, the more enjoyable the journey will be. When we do this, it helps us be more compassionate and curious with ourselves, enabling us to gain momentum and experience more growth. My mentor, Dr. Allen McCray, gave me a golden nugget of wisdom the day I began working with him. He said, "you cannot speed up the process, but you can slow it down."

I took that as a challenge, as I was hell-bent on not slowing my process down, doing all I could do on my side, and taking full responsibility for my growth. At the time, I was more focused on not slowing it down, but now I understand the importance of not speeding up the process. Because it's in the process where we become, that who we become in the process is far more rewarding than actually reaching the goal or destination itself.

> *"You cannot speed up the process,*
> *but you can slow it down".*
> *— Allen McCray*

———•••●●••———

Remember the movies like Romancing the Stone and Goonies (any other 80's movie buffs out there?)? They are two great classics with this common theme: they are both built around the storyline of acquiring a treasure map, which leads to a treasure. In these movies, the first focus is on the treasure map and all the benefits they will receive when they reach and obtain the fortune.

But, as with life, the real gift is what they learn about themselves, the cultivated relationships, and who they became in the adventure of finding the treasure.

Who you become in the process of where you want to go is more important than reaching the goal. It's in becoming that you truly realize who you are and become the person who can sustain where you are going and what you want to achieve.

For this book, and getting a visual for the process, we will tap into treasure maps. What does a treasure map consist of? It has an X where the treasure lies. It has the steps of how to get there, filled with clues, landmarks, and a path. With your adventurist living treasure map, each point and location that leads to your treasure (your goal) will require different tools that will work together to get you to your destination – all of this unlocks your adventurist living mindset.

Allowing the idea of your life being an adventure, like in the movies mentioned, awaken something in you. Think about when you are watching these types of movies. When it's a good movie, you can feel as though you are on that roller coaster adventure with them, like you are in the movie with them!

I don't know about you, but part of me wished I could experience the exciting life they were in the movie! What if that could be real? Becoming alive, taking chances, going after something big. My logical side, limiting beliefs, and the internal story I was telling myself, all too quickly, bring me to a halt. My limiting beliefs were all chanting in unison that the adventure that was calling from the well deep inside me could never really be my reality, that it was childish. Grow up, Felicia.

What a lie.

The lie is that adventure is only calling to some of us. That it is limited and only exists in some of the elite, the chosen, the lucky ones. I truly believe that adventure lies within every one of us. It can just look different. The wonderful thing about adventure is that it is unique to each of us.

We will keep reiterating the concept that adventure, adventurist living, is experiencing unknown and new territory in each area of your life daily. I will keep saying it because they (who are they, not sure) say it takes us being exposed to something six or more before we get it.

What this all boils down to is that adventure is growth.

When we are growing, becoming, and experiencing the new and unknown territory that challenges our limiting beliefs, our ceilings, and our limitations, this is where we encounter our unique adventure and feel most alive.

In the movie Romancing the Stone, Joan Wilder, a famous mousy, timid romance novelist, sets off for Columbia to pay the ransom for her kidnapped sister. She soon finds herself in the middle of a dangerous adventure hunting for treasure with a mercenary rogue (of course, he becomes her love interest), and her life takes a shift.

She was famous, but she was stuck. She lived through the romance novels she wrote. She lived in a fantasy that was separate from herself. This is how a lot of the world lives. I know I was. In our current generation, in addition to movies and shows, there's the illusion that we are experiencing life through other people's social media, through their unrealistic filters, through the idea that they have the life we want, but we ourselves can't have. Since that will never satisfy our unique adventure calling from within us, what happens? We binge even more on social media, Netflix, Hulu, games, shopping, or anything that will distract us or numbs us from really living our lives.

Back to Joan Wilder. She hardly ever left her New York apartment, and her cat was her main companion (no judgment for the cat ladies out there!). She was shut down, uncolorful, drab – her outward countenance spoke of her inner condition. She was hiding.

Where adventure stories begin can vary, some are stuck or not living life, as in Joan Wilder's case, and some are going through challenging circumstances, as with the Goonies. Regardless of where the story starts, it begins with an opportunity, an invitation. There's never a question about it;

adventure is always calling out. The real question is, how and will you respond?

The adventurist living mindset is not limited to what most would typically categorize adventure as, for example, trekking through the jungles of Columbia (Romancing the Stone), backpacking through Europe, hiking Machu Picchu, or summiting Mount Everest. Yes, those kinds of adventures are exhilarating.

But don't allow yourself to limit adventure and confine it to exist only within the boxes you may have created when the truth is that you can experience adventure every day of your life in your everyday living. Each day you're presented with an invitation and an opportunity to embrace and pursue your unique adventure. When you grasp this truth, that you exploring new and unknown territory (growth) is adventure, this is where life becomes fresh, invigorating, you have more energy, and where more of your days become "the best day of your life."

In what areas is adventure available? Here are just some listed to help you begin picturing what adventure would like in these different areas of life:

- Relationships

- Friendships

- Spiritual Walk

- Health and Wellness

- Careers and Purpose

- Finances and Wealth

- Education and Developing Skills

- Hobbies

- Fun and Recreation

- Serving and Contributing to the World

- Home and Office Environment

- The Overall Mantra or Banner of Your Life

- And any other area you want to add or comes to mind

The adventure mindset is that you were created to be learning and growing in all areas of your life and everyday life.

Each day you're presented with an invitation and an opportunity to embrace and pursue your unique adventure.

———————•••●●•••———————

When we learn and grow every day, we move out of our comfort zone and into what I call the Adventure Zone.

A disclaimer early, does this all happen effortlessly, seamlessly, and precisely as planned? That would be a great big nope. Growth and going beyond your comfort zone and into your Adventure Zone takes work, intentionality, and will come with its challenges, as any great adventure does. The obstacles and bumps in your journey are, in fact, crucial to your adventure story. It is in those times where you will grow, be stretched, and become more of your true self if you remain committed to the process and keep your eye on where you want to go.

If you make up your mind that you are going to extract every ounce of life, growth, and experience out of your everyday living, that is where you begin to experience life passionately. After time, that mindset becomes who you are and your lifestyle. And isn't that what we all want when it boils down to it? To deeply experience this one and only life we've been given?

In your adventure, that treasure you're going after isn't something minuscule. It is your life. It is worth pursuing. This book will serve as your treasure map, and it will help give you the tools (landmarks) to move you forward on your journey. There will be ups and downs, uncomfortable and exciting times, times you want to give up, and times you feel like you could fly. It's rarely a straight shot.

If you need to stay a little while at one of the stops, do it. Extract all you need to, and then continue. These steps are meant to become a part of your life, applied and revisited.

If you have made up your mind that you will go after it no matter what, do the work, live the life you were created to, you've already begun your adventure! Congratulations!

This is your adventure. It won't look like anyone else's. Own it. It's yours.

Ah-ha's and Discovery

How do you feel about beginning your adventure?

_____

_____

_____

The picture that you were given is a tangible treasure map. What would the treasure at the end be for you? What goal or experience would excite your soul to go after?

_____

_____

_____

You know that with any adventure worth taking, there will be ups and downs. How do you want to face those ups and downs? How do you want to show up?

_____

_____

_____

Moving forward in your life and truly living your life is worth the risk!

YOUR WHOLE LIFE ADVENTURE:
THE LIFE WHEEL

"So please ask yourself: What would I do if I weren't afraid? And then go do it."
- Sheryl Sandberg

A re you ready to officially get started on your adventurist living journey?!

I have laid some foundation, and what you will continue to learn will all build off of one another. Now you are more prepared to begin. Preparation is important, but the truth is you can only prepare so much, and then you have to get out there! The rest can only be learned in the experience.

Let's use the treasure map analogy some more.

As we've already talked about, there is always a big "X" represented on treasure maps that reflects "this is where the treasure is!". That X is our goal, our destination. Okay, you know where you want to go, but you may need clarity on where you are now, in the present moment. You have to find your "You are here" location to have an accurate *reality* of where you are starting. This can sometimes be the "not so fun part." It takes courage to give an accurate and honest assessment of where you are, but it is necessary. You can't have instructions or a plan to get somewhere until you know where you are starting from.

Self-evaluation is key to growing and learning. This is what adventurist living is all about. If you can change your mindset from avoiding evaluating yourself to embracing it and practicing it, you will begin to learn to love it. You will learn to love it because you are taking personal responsibility for your life and its direction and learn how it will powerfully display itself in your life.

An excellent tool to find clarity on where you are right now in your life and to assess the areas of your life you want to begin focusing your energy to work on is the wheel of life. I am not the creator of the wheel of life, but it is very useful, and why recreate the wheel? Pun intended.

Self-evaluation is key to growing and learning.

———————•••● ●••———————

The wheel of life is intended to be used to give you the picture view of your life, a lot like a helicopter that can hover and provide the bigger perspective, the wheel of life will help you to see where you are in the main areas that make up the totality of your life.

Without awareness of your whole life, you will tend to unconsciously focus on 1-2 areas while the other areas of life are lived in automatic pilot, neglect, and reaction. It's important to take inventory of your whole life, to make intentional choices and goals in each area.

You are going to do your Wheel of Life in this chapter! Yay! Before beginning, put on your compassion and curiosity. This exercise is not meant to make you feel bad about yourself or where you are. Shift your mindset to being proud of yourself for doing it and getting real about where you are, and intentional about where you want to go.

Many people I work with tend to beat themselves up for their wheel of life results initially. However, when they begin shifting their mindset to being proud of themselves for making the moves to get real about where they are so they can make a plan for where they want to go, it changes their experience.

Below is an example of the Wheel of Life Circle:

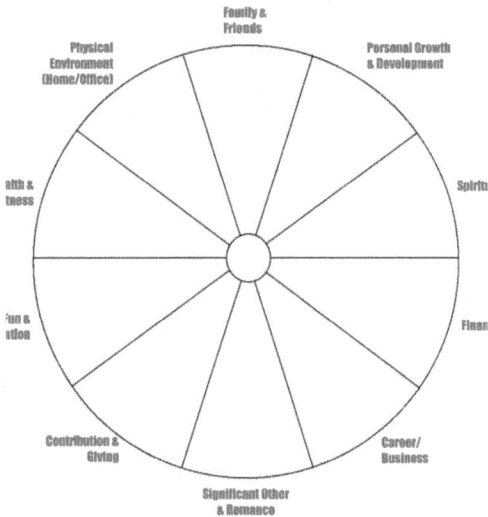

Take time and fill out your wheel of life. When filling out this circle, focus on where you are RIGHT NOW, not where you want to be. Get real with yourself. Fill it out on a scale of 1-10. The inner smaller circle represents "0," and the outer circle represents "10". You can go to https://adventurlistliving.com/bookresources to download and print one for yourself or draw a circle and create your wheel of life.

With the wheel, feel free to change the name(s) of the areas to what speaks to you directly and add areas if you'd like. The importance is to realize many areas make up your life. By looking at them individually, you gain more clarity and get to make intentional decisions and goals for each area.

Here is an example of a wheel filled out by one of my clients, who we will call Rachel:

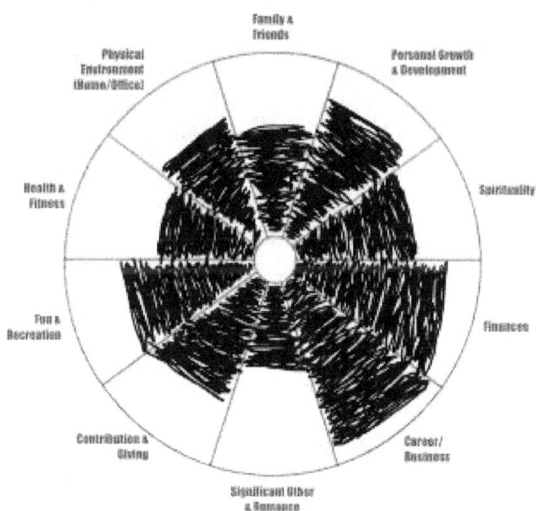

If you were to take the outer circle away and use the shaded-in area, which represented the wheel that would take you through life, it would be pretty bumpy and make for a rough ride through life. Here is an example of what it looks like:

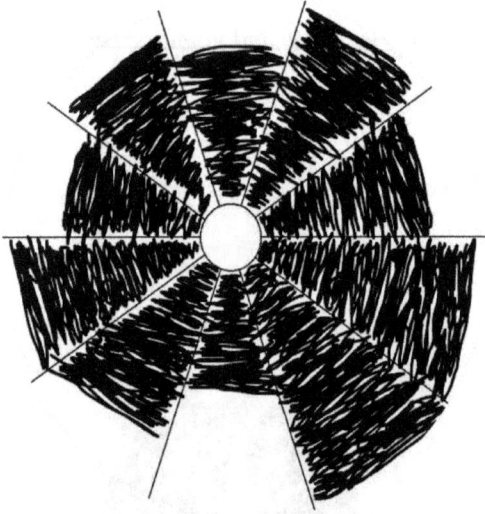

After Rachel completed her wheel of life, she felt like many people can after they do this exercise for the first time. She felt terrible about her honest results.

If that's you, keep reading.

This exercise is not meant to make you feel bad, quite the contrary. Its purpose is to bring to your awareness the reality of where you think you are in life. Guess what, you were already there, now you are just aware of it. That is a great place to be because you cannot change and assess anything you are not aware of. Let's unpack how to use this tool.

Back to Rachel. Once she got past feeling bad, by doing some deep breathing and embraced that this was a pretty accurate reflection of her life, I asked her, "looking at your wheel, what is it telling you about your life right now?". She replied it was imbalanced, and she could see how she needed a lot of work, specifically in health and fitness and a significant other (romance).

The next question I asked was what she could find to celebrate that her wheel results showed her? She paused and thought for a while. It is always easier for people to focus on their shortcomings than celebrating wins, strengths, and what has been accomplished. She said, "hmmm... well, I have worked very hard at my career and, as a result, have become a very successful business owner, which in return has also made a positive impact on my finances. I am now the first person in my family to #1: be an entrepreneur and #2: break the poverty cycle." When she said that out loud, she was surprised, how

good it felt to celebrate her wins and said, "wow, I did that!".
Now, that's cool.

When you look at your wheel of life, what can you celebrate right now? If you're having a hard time at first, let me help you out. You can honor that you took the time, energy, and intention and the step to complete your wheel of life and got real with yourself. That alone is worth celebrating. Remember how celebrating was one of the tools that you packed to begin and use on your journey? Revisit that if needed and put your celebration practices into practice!

When Rachel replaced self-condemnation and self-judgment with self-compassion, curiosity, and celebration and assessed her wheel of life from that state of mind, it changed her entire experience. She went from feeling bad about herself to feeling good about knowing where she was in life right and that she had the power to make the plan for change in her life.

This is one of the steps in taking personal responsibility for your life. It takes courage to get real and assess your life where you, and that is where the magic begins. When you know where you are, and set goals, transformation and life take place. Now, you can create action steps to get you to your destination.

I asked Rachel to focus on two areas of her life that she wanted to allot most of her energy to in the next quarter. She chose health/wellness and romance, which in her case, were the two areas with the lowest shaded in area on her wheel.

That doesn't have to be the case for you. You get to decide. It's your wheel of life. It's your life to choose what you want to work on now intentionally. Let me give you another example with Mike's experience.

Mike was going to school for his MBA. He was on a pathway to complete his schooling a year sooner than it takes most. Consequently, he had a large school load. On his wheel of life, his personal growth and development were the highest out of any other area. Understandably, his life was consumed with school, and that is where the majority of his energy was spent, and he was alright with that. He owned it. He knew for the next couple of years, his wheel of life would reflect that.

Although the lowest area on his wheel was fun and recreation, he consciously made his goals from his wheel results and continued giving most of his energy to schoolwork. He wasn't going to give most of his energy to fun and recreation during school, but he set a manageable goal that didn't require too much of his energy to schedule something fun two hours a week to improve his mental health and lower stress. So that small goal, which he hadn't given thought to until seeing his wheel of life results, will not only impact his energy for school and give him some enjoyment but will also improve his overall health.

I will get into the adventures of goal setting in a later chapter. But I do encourage people to set their goals based on their wheel of life. This is setting value-based goals. Meaning you are setting your goals intentionally on what is important to you.

I redo my wheel of life and revisit setting new goals every quarter. Here is a visual I use when evaluating my current wheel of life results and setting goals, and deciding the amount of energy I am putting towards each goal.

I picture a 4-burner stove. The two front burners represent the two goals I want to focus most of my time and energy on. Usually, this is because they are the most challenging goals. These are the goals that create the most growth.

The two back burners represent goals that I am pursuing and require some effort, but not as much as the two front burner goals. They are where something is simmering, and eventually, it will be brought to the front burners. The goals these burners represent do require attention and action but are not that challenging, and simple steps improve them in significant ways.

Then there are my kitchen cabinets above the burner. This is where I have put goals (consciously) that I will be working on in the future, but for now, I am not investing my time, energy and focus on them.

I am a salsa dancer. I love salsa and will reference it since I have learned so much from it. I have been dancing for over four years now, and there are no signs of me falling less in love. I am more in love with it today than ever before.

For the first three years of dancing, I danced six times a week. That is a lot of evenings out for this early riser, but I knew I wanted to grow in my skill. So, I took a lot of classes, got a lot of one-on-one training, and practiced my skills out in the real world, often asking someone to dance that was way beyond my skill level.

When I would do my wheel of life during this time, my life's fun and recreation area ranked at a nice high 9 ½. Other higher areas in my life would be health/wellness and relationships. My two front burners were my salsa goals and my health/wellness goals. The areas I felt I was at a 5 or lower at that time were: finances/money and romantic relationships.

And I was okay with that because it was intentional.

After those initial three years, I did my wheel again, like I always do every quarter, and decided it was time to take salsa off one of the front burners. Right now, it's in the cupboard for this season. Does that mean I have stopped dancing? Nooo. No way. I love it too much. What that means is that I am not using the majority of my time, energy and focus on growing in it at this time. I will decide in the future when it will make its way out of the cupboard and back onto the stove. Make sense?

I also moved health and fitness to the back burner. I have hit many of my goals in this area, but it is always something that I want to actively work on since it's necessary to live a long, healthy, and vibrant life. What has made it to the front-burner status, you ask? That would be finance/money and career. With romantic relationships hanging out health/wellness on the back burners.

Now that you've done your wheel of life begin to evaluate your life. Where do you want to go? What does it look like? And what is your life wheel revealing about where you want to start? Remember, adventurist living is all about exploring new and unknown territory. Where do you want to begin in your life today? What areas do you want to focus on in this season? This year?

Do the following work and continue on your adventurist living journey! It's worth it, and you're worth it!

Ah-ha's and Discovery

How do you feel when you see your wheel of life results?

_____

_____

_____

What were the areas that surprised you and why?

_____

_____

_____

What does it look like to look at your wheel of life having compassion and curiosity with yourself?

_____

_____

_____

And... ACTION!

What are the two areas you do want to put on your front burners and focus most of your time and energy on right now? The areas you know that will also be the most challenging for you?

_____

_____

_____

IT BEGINS WITH A DREAM.

———•◆•———

"Nothing happens, unless first a dream."
– Carl Sandburg

———••●●••———

For some people dreaming and imagination come easily. More than likely, this was cultivated, supported, and encouraged in your development years. You were encouraged to dream, imagine, be free. You felt supported, loved, and safe. But, for some of us. It isn't that easy to dream.

The restrictions in dreaming can be a result of the environment we were raised in. Maybe we had critical parents or caregivers. It could be a traumatic event or events that we experienced, and we were forced to live in survival mode. Whatever the reason may be or when it occurred, your dream and imagination life may have been shut down or limited. That was some of my story. I grew up in a volatile household, where my parents were fighting what seemed 24/7, both physically and emotionally abusive to one another. My father, who was an Army drill sergeant, could also be very critical and harsh. They both did the best they could do, as most parents do, but they were limited to their own experiences and limitations in their parenting. The result as a child was that my dream life was completely locked up. My reality kept me living in my reality. But, we can begin to dream again – it's in our make-up and nature to do so.

As children, we were created to dream easily and to do so without hesitation or even thought – it is natural. It's how we are made. Then, as adults, we are told to grow up, get our heads out of the clouds. We're advised to be realistic, to be responsible, and put our childish imagination away.

We were not created to abandon our imagination. It's in our imagination where we begin to unlock our full potential, download ideas that reveal our true passions and purpose, set big goals, come up with solutions, dream up ideas and become our most authentic and best selves.

If you feel shut down when it comes to dreaming and using your imagination – do not worry. First, be encouraged that you are not alone, and second, it's never too late! You can begin unlocking and awakening your imagination and your dreams now.

Remember the open-minded exercise? When you are practicing being open-minded, engaging your imagination, this opens up a sea of possibilities.

When I think about those who embraced imagination, I instantly think about Albert Einstein. He has so many awesome quotes about imagination. What's interesting, usually, when we think about science, we think all logic and facts. We think that science and a healthy imagination would conflict quite the contrary. It was Einstein's incredible imagination and his appreciation for it that not only made him the Nobel Peace Prize winning scientist he was but also a genius inventor. It was from his imagination that ideas were birthed. Because of this, he was able to discover, achieve and bring so much to the world in his lifetime.

When you are practicing being open-minded,

you are engaging your imagination,

this opens up a sea of possibilities.

Before we get into some exercises to help us unlock and begin awakening our imaginations, I want to share some of Einstein's quotes that may help fuel the fire of your inspiration. to begin to imagine and dream. Make notes, circle, or even write the ones that speak to you somewhere you can see it every day.

"Imagination is more important than knowledge. Imagination is the language of the soul. Pay attention to your imagination, and you will discover all you need to be fulfilled."

"Logic will get you from A to B. Imagination will take you everywhere."

"Imagination is everything. It is the preview of life's coming attractions."

"If you want your children to be intelligent, read them fairytales. If you want your children to be more intelligent, read them more fairytales."

"The true sign of intelligence is not knowledge, but imagination."

Cultivating Your Imagination

Cultivating your imagination is like any skill. It takes intentionality, practice and it is developed over time. For a lot of people, when beginning to utilize their imagination and dreaming, they get stuck. As mentioned before, this can be a result of many different things. Regardless of the reason, regardless of age, you can begin unlocking your imagination and dream life again regardless of your current circumstances.

Remember to continue to treat yourself with compassion and curiosity as you begin and go through this process. If you get stuck, take a moment, step back and return when you're ready. But return.

Cultivating Your imagination is like any skill.
It takes intentionality, practice and it is developed
over time.

———————•••● ●••———————

Here are some exercises and challenges to help open up the creative, imaginative well that does reside within you.

The first three exercises were adapted from a TEDxMileHigh article by Kendra Sand:

Seek Adventure (talking my language!)

Seeking adventure means experiencing new things. In this case, adventure can look like planning a trip, taking a drawing, writing, ax-throwing, shooting, dance, art, cooking class, etc. Teach yourself how to juggle on YouTube, take an online course, or wander your city (without a map app). Create your adventure!

Play

Imagination is a natural state for children. Kids spend up to two-thirds of their time in imaginative play. Imaginative play is played out in non-reality; it requires seeing things not as they are but as they could be on any planet or galaxy. This kind of play sometimes appears as a loss of self-control and rational thinking.

Spend an hour in imaginative play. Permit yourself to safely let go of the aspects of adult life and embrace non-reality. If you need a little help with imaginative play, here are some suggestions:

Start in nature and let yourself imagine anything wild that comes to mind.

Connect with your inner child through prayer, meditation, or journaling and revisit some of your earliest imaginations. I remember my sister and I once dug a hole in our backyard and swore we had made it to China!

Read novels of speculative fiction and magical realism.

Star Gaze

Stargazing is an ancient practice that inspired many thinkers, creatives, and dreamers. With the invention of electricity and pollution, most of us don't have the daily opportunity to gaze at the stars (well, at least gaze and be able to see them). But this kind of wondering is important. It's intergalactic wondering.

Try to get to a place where you can see the stars. Get out of town and gaze away. Another way you can do this is by taking a visit to a planetarium.

Dream Inventory

Dream inventory is an exercise that I do in my self-leadership and goal-setting workshops. It's this simple.

Sit down and write as many dreams as you can. Aim for coming up with fifty dreams. This doesn't have to be done all at once, and you can revisit it as many times as you need to.

As part of my quarterly life wheel process, I also include adding to my dream inventory. Just in case, because some have asked before, these are our "awake" dreams we are talking about, not the dreams we experience when asleep.

When it comes to doing a dream inventory, you may get stuck at first. That's okay! Write as many dreams as you can now and keep revisiting them. Here are a few ways that may help you when tapping in and creating your dream list:

Time, space, and money do not matter.

You are not limited to time, space or money when it comes to your dreams. It doesn't matter your age, your financial situation, where you live, or your past. Dream as if you were Walt Disney creating your own movie! For example, one of my dreams is that I can fly!

You have a billion dollars.

What would you do? What would your experience be? Who would you help? What would you build? What would you buy?

No dream is too big OR too small.

Don't judge your dreams. They are yours, whatever they are, write them down and express them. Utilizing your imagination allows your dreams to flow out of the well within you. They are in there wanting to come out!

Dreams are not your goals.

Don't think that all of your dreams need to come to pass. They are not your goals and don't have to happen. When we begin noting our dreams, they can show us a pattern or insight into our true passions. For example, one of my dreams is to provide education to every child on the planet to receive an education and learn self-leadership skills. Another dream of mine is to own a house or cottage on every single island in the world. Another is to give business loans (specifically to women) to entrepreneurs in developing countries.

Now, get your journal (hopefully, you've already begun one for your journey through this book) and start jotting down your dreams. Decide that you're going to make this exercise enjoyable. Have fun unlocking your childlike imagination and see what's deep in you!

Cultivating your imagination is a process. Continue to be intentional about doing exercises that nourish your imagination and dream life. Keep on looking at your dream inventory and adding to it. **Your imagination doesn't have an end date or ever run out.** It is something you can access daily to unlock the ideas, solutions, and vibrancy of your adventurous life.

Ah-ha's and Discovery

What did you dream about as a child?

_____

_____

_____

Where did you believe your imagination was at the beginning of this chapter?

_____

_____

_____

What was your experience in writing down your dreams?

_____

_____

_____

Did you see any patterns in your dreams? What were they?

_____

_____

_____

And... ACTION!

Which exercises are you going to incorporate to cultivate your imagination?

_____

_____

_____

When are you going to do the exercises you chose above?

_____

_____

_____

Look at your dream inventory daily.

Keep adding to your dream inventory until you reach at least fifty dreams. Create a time when you add to your dreams, monthly, quarterly, annually, or any time you choose.

Goals: The "X" on Your Treasure Map

"*Without dreams and goals, there is no living, only existing and that is not why we are here.*"
– *Mark Twain*

Remember how we talked about the treasure map of our lives? What do all treasure maps have? They have that big ole "X" that marks where the treasure lies! Think of a goal, your goal(s), as the X on your treasure map. It's a symbol of where you want to go.

Why are goals so important?

Can you imagine a treasure map without the "X"? Imagine someone giving you a map without a destination. You'd be like, "Ummm, so where's the X? Where are we going?"

This is why goals are essential and necessary to live life to the fullest and grow and become, why they are vitally important to living out the adventure mindset.

Your goals are what call you out into that unknown and new territory, where you live a life of growing, learning, and developing every day. Without goals, we can end up living on autopilot or out of reaction to everything around us. This is taking on the lifestyle that life is happening "to us" rather than life is happening "for us." This is the opposite of intentional living. Intentional living is pulling out that treasure map every day (even more if necessary) and looking at that X and saying, "this is where I am heading towards today" and "what steps do I take today that move me towards my goal.

This is a different approach to life than waking up and living Groundhog's Day every day, which, unfortunately, for most people is their entire life unless they choose to wake up to life and decide to live it on purpose. For a lot of people, everyday life may look a little something like this:"

Get up.

Shower.

Eat breakfast.

Quick interactions with spouse and children.

Off to school and drop-off.

Off to work.

Work all day, waiting for it to be over.

Get off of work.

Get kids.

Possibly a workout.

Eat dinner.

Watch TV.

Go to sleep.

Wake up and do it all over again. And of course, within all of those interactions, be on the phone mindlessly scrolling through other people's lives instead of living their own. And hopefully, have enough put away in retirement to get through the rest of life until death. That sounds great, right? No, it doesn't. Not for me, and I would guess that if you've stayed with me to this point, it doesn't to you either!

I don't know about you, but the idea of living my entire life (or any part of it actually) in automatic pilot now scares the crap out of me in a good way. It's a reverence for this life, for time and how precious it is, and that we only get one try at this life. I want to squeeze every ounce of energy out of it, love deeply, leave an impact and legacy and at the end of it say, "what a ride, I have no regrets."

> *Without goals, we can end up living on autopilotor*
> *out of reaction to everything around us.*

———————••●●●●••———————

Maybe you've bought into the "American Dream" concept, where an annual vacation or any chances you get to "get away from your regular life" are the highlights of your year. Maybe you've believed they are your only opportunities for your adventurous moments in life. They are what you look forward to. And then once you have taken your trip, your escape, you wait all year long for your next vacation.

There is that word…wait.

So many of us are waiting for life to happen. We are waiting for that next special event, waiting to start or waiting for something to happen to us. Too many people have bought into the lie that life cannot be exciting and adventurous every day. Whether you're single, married, widowed, divorced, retired, a student, a child, whatever your status, age, background, I believe we were created to experience adventure every…single…day.

If we don't set goals and establish an aim, a focus, we end up being guided and tossed in response to everything happening around us.

Here is a visual to think about as it pertains to your goals, an additional visual to the X on your treasure map. When we set goals, what we have created is a target. Picture yourself as an archer. You have your bow and your arrows. The bow represents your mindset, and the arrows represent your decisions and your actions. You have your bullseye, and that sweet center circle is your goal.

Without a bullseye you would either choose to hold onto your arrows and not shoot at all (which you were made to take action) or choose to shoot out into nothing, which is shooting in reaction to life. You would end up hitting nothing at all and become good at it. When living life without a target and continuing to live in reaction, it's tiring, it's dull, it's overwhelming, it's unsatisfying, and it's not moving you anywhere.

But when you have a bullseye, you take a deep breath in, you are focused, and have a clear vision of where you are going, and begin making the moves to get there. Clarity is powerful. Picture a bullseye right now. As you focus on that inner circle, it becomes "IPhone 11 portrait clear" (I know I just lost a lot of Android users right now – okay, you guys have great cameras!), and everything else fades away in comparison. You're not looking at everything else around the target. You are lasered in on the center circle.

When you begin going after your goals, does it come easy? Do you shoot your first arrow and hit the center effortlessly? Unless you have some super beginner's luck, the odds are no.

With any challenging and worthwhile goal, it will take steps and action, it will take practice to get there, and it will require getting out of your comfort zone. Don't despise being a beginner, instead honor and enjoy the process. Make the decision you will embrace the learning and the process, and yes, it will come with challenges, but it's worth it.

S.M.A.R.T. Goals

I did not create the S.M.A.R.T. goal method, but it works. It's a great tool to get started setting your goals now and to use in the future.

S.M.A.R.T. stands for the following:

S – Specific

M – Measurable

A – Achievable

R – Relevant

T – Timely or Timebound

Let's break those down individually, so you can begin putting some X's on your map and creating some bullseyes!

Specific.

For a goal to be a goal, it needs to be specific. Think about it like this, how would you know you've hit the goal? The "specific" would be that bullseye, not the outer parts of it.

I work with people with their health and wellness goals. When we begin our conversation, I ask them what their goal is, and a majority of them say something to the effect of "to be healthy." This is not a specific goal because it doesn't address what they would need to do to become healthy or what being healthy would look like for them. To help them get clear and specific about their goal, I ask, "how would you know you have hit your goal of being healthy? What would have to happen?".

Some answers I've been given are "I would be able to get off my diabetes or blood pressure medicine," "Losing 100 pounds", "being able to run a 10k", "playing with grandkids for an hour and not be winded," etc.

You can see how these are specific because it's clear on what is to be accomplished. You would know when you have achieved the goal.

Another "S" word to be combined with being specific is stretching. Our goals should challenge us and grow us. If a goal is easy, it really isn't a goal. When creating a specific and stretching goal, it should scare us a little. Then, we can make smaller steps within that goal to get there.

Measurable.

This means you have a way of evaluating and tracking your progress and success. How will you know when you have reached your goal? What are your benchmarks?

Using the examples of health goals given before: no longer needing diabetic and high blood pressure medications, losing that 100 pounds, running that 10K, building the stamina to play with the grandchildren for an hour and not be winded. Benchmark examples could be: for diabetes, sugar levels improving month-to-month, losing 10 pounds every 8-weeks for the weight loss, gradually increasing the distance of running weekly for the 10k and incorporating and steadily increasing cardio into their life, maybe 10-minutes, three times a week and then next month 15-minutes, four times a week and so on for the grandparent wanting to play with their grandchildren.

How can you measure the steps toward your goal along the way?

Achievable.

Is your goal attainable and not impossible to achieve? This will help you figure out ways you can realize your goal and work towards it. The goal should make you feel challenged, but understanding the difference between being challenged and not being achievable.

Example: I am a 5'2" woman. I may love basketball, and out of my love for basketball, I decide it makes sense to become a professional WNBA player. Even with the greatest coaches and trainers, the odds are that I will not achieve my goal of becoming a professional basketball player. Make sense?

Another example: Did you ever watch American Idol? Did you see when they would show the auditions of the people that literally had no singing ability? Did that make anyone else uncomfortable watching (I know it did me)? Those people had the ambition and goals to become singing superstars, but based on their singing ability displayed, it's more than likely it will not be achievable.

Relevant.

This is where you want to get real and ask yourself the question, "does this goal line up with who I am? Is it realistic and in line with my life purpose?" Is this the right time to pursue this goal? Being relevant boils down to purpose and timing.

With any of your goals, you want first to make sure that they are yours. Not what your parents may have wanted for you, your family, friends, spouse, or even what society or your culture has suggested for you.

With any challenging and worthwhile goal,
it will take steps and action, it will take practice to
get there, and it will require getting out of your
comfort zone.

---•••●•••---

For example, my sister-in-law Lori was told her whole life that she would be an excellent grade school teacher because she was great with kids. She ended up taking on that goal as her own and went to college to become a teacher. After all, what profession could be more honorable? Being responsible for helping to teach and mold precious little kiddos and the future leaders of the world? That has to be a good goal.

A ton of school debt later and four years of her life spent, she completed her college degree and became a kindergarten teacher. She hated it.

She had taken on the identity and the goals that others had imposed on her. Who is responsible for her doing this? She is. We are all accountable for our own decisions and for taking ownership of our own goals.

Guess what she ended up doing? She had always been drawn to this particular candle shop in Kansas. She loved their candles and had gotten to know the owner from her frequent trips to her shop. Through time and conversations, an idea of a franchise was birthed. She set the goal to open a candle shop franchise in Kansas City, Missouri, and she did it. Now, she loves what she's doing, and she is very good at it! Twenty years later and it is a successful and thriving business!

That is because it was her goal, her passion.

Once you have established your goal is relevant, next ask yourself, is now the right time? You may have a goal to travel more or take a specific trip that has been on your bucket list for years. But, right now, you have a goal to complete grad school, which requires most of your time and energy.

The goal to take that trip is still worthwhile and in line with your long-term objectives. However, now may not be the right time. This could be a goal you put in the kitchen cabinet to revisit later on down the road.

I believe there is a goal or focus that is always relevant, and that is with our health and wellness. If your health and body are not in a good place, it's a good idea to make that a priority—our health and how we feel impacts every other area of our lives. It's harder to reach those other goals if you are always tired, bed-ridden, don't feel good about yourself, and unhealthy. Not to get too extreme, but it's true, you can't do anything if you're dead.

Timely.

You have to put a timeline and a date to your goal. As the quote by Milton Erickson so accurately says: "A goal without a date is just a dream."

A target date is what puts fuel to your fire, motivates you, and gets you moving. Without this, you will continue to keep pushing the action necessary to make your goal a reality tomorrow or later. You can keep saying you have the goal, but without a target date, weeks pass, months pass, years pass, decades pass, and you at the end of your life wish you had accomplished that goal. You never had a deadline, a date to your goal.

I am drawn to the word deadline when it comes to setting a date for goals. It gives more of the sense of how important a date is. It has an added element of firmness and necessity, doesn't it? I shifted to using that word while writing this book. I realized that when I worked for others, I met my deadlines in the corporate setting or even in the non-profit sector. I would work day and night, after hours, to meet the deadlines given me. I also had this tenacity when it came to actual events (retreats, workshops, camps, etc.) where there is a date and people were showing up. I always met each one of those goals by the date given.

I began thinking to myself, what if I put deadlines to my goals and gave the same grit, determination, and persistence to reach the deadlines of the goals that mattered to me? It has been a game-changer, and why you are reading this book right now instead of a rough draft sitting in my documents never released to the world to read.

A target date is what puts fuel to your fire, motivates you, and gets you moving. Without this, you will constantly keep pushing the action necessary to make your goal a reality to tomorrow or later.

•••●•••

Once you have set a timeline to accomplish your goal, ask yourself when I will work on this goal? Daily? Weekly? Which days of the week? What hours? Get very specific regarding the time you are scheduling to work on your goal. I call this my needle-mover time. This is when I am moving the needle towards my goals. This can be a real game-changer in obtaining your goals and making them a reality.

Now that you know what S.M.A.R.T. goals are, it's time to set goals. Suppose you're having a hard time coming up with goals. Remember the wheel of life chapter? Go back to your wheel of life and pick two areas where you want to start.

Use the S.M.A.R.T. goal template example on the next page to answer the questions for each one of your goals. You can also

download   and   print   this   template   at
https://adventuristinglivingbook.com/bookresources.

GOAL: _____

TODAY'S DATE: _____

S	SPECIFIC	-What do I want to accomplish? -Why do I want to accomplish this? -What are the requirements?	
M	MEASURABLE	-How will I measure my progress? -How will I know when the goal has been accomplished?	
A	ACHIEVABLE	-How can the goal be accomplished? -What are the steps to be taken to accomplish the goal?	
R	RELEVANT	-Is this a worthwhile goal? -Is this the right time? -Is this goal in line with my long-term objectives?	
T	TIMELY	-When is the completion of this goal due? -When am I going to work on this goal?	

This is part of your journey to living your adventurist life. You get to set goals that challenge you, and that's where the adventure starts to become unlocked. Your goals should scare you a little! If you're feeling some anxiety, that's normal!

Anxiety and excitement are part of the same emotion. It's just a matter of how you interpret it! You can say this is giving me anxiety or this is exciting me—your choice.

Set goals that are big enough to get your breathing going and have you saying to yourself, "wow, I am doing this!".

Keep this in mind when setting goals and pursuing them. The process and the journey are more important than reaching the goal itself. Our goals are meant to teach and grow us. If you were to achieve our goals immediately, easily, or prematurely, you wouldn't have the opportunity to experience growth and learn from them. It's in the learning and growing that you become the person that is necessary to sustain the goal. Through the process, you become and continue to become a better version of yourself.

Let's take lottery winners, for example. Why do people play the lottery? They desire to be more financially secure, to not worry about money anymore, to be able to do more things, take care of their family, etc.

Did you know it is estimated that around 90% of lottery winners end up bankrupt just a few years after receiving a large sum of money? In addition to that, there have been countless stories of how it has destroyed families, caused depression and suicide. Some winners have said they did not like who they had become after winning.

The problem with the lottery is that the recipients receive a fortune immediately.

> *It's in the learning and growing that you become the person that is necessary to sustain the goal.*

---•••●●•••---

There was no process of who they needed to become to be the person who knows how to manage wealth. They brought all of their values and beliefs into their win, which more than likely, were the same values and beliefs that kept them living paycheck to paycheck and possibly with a poverty mindset. They were still that same person bringing those values and beliefs into their lottery winning experience.

Even though they reached their goal of having more money, they had not become the person needed to sustain the wealth. And even going further beyond that, them becoming the person who could continue to build more wealth. That is what happens when we attain our goal without the process.

Another example we can see this in is losing weight quickly with crash diets.

One of my best friend's mom began a broccoli and tuna crash diet because she wanted to lose weight quickly. All I recall is that those were the two main items she could eat for an entire two-week timeframe.

Did she lose a lot of weight quickly? Yes. Did she keep that weight off? What do you think?

No, she did not. For one, sustaining that kind of food lifestyle is not realistic. I remember I did it with her for three of those days and was so sick of broccoli and tuna! That experience made me stay away from those two items for almost a year!

More importantly, she hadn't become the person and adopted the mindset and the discipline necessary to make eating healthy a habit and a lifestyle.

IT'S TIME TO WORK

Setting your goals is the first step, and now it's time to put the work into making them a reality. Yes, it will take work. I am not going to pretend that going after your goals is easy. If the goal is worth pursuing, it's going to be challenging. Prepare yourself to do the work. It will be uncomfortable because nothing great ever happens in our comfort zone. You can choose to despise or embrace the process.

The people you admire for going after their dreams and goals, trust me, they are putting in the work. Most of the time, we only see the fruits of their labor and not all of the background action, challenges, blood, sweat, and tears of what it took to get there.

It will be uncomfortable because nothing great
ever happens in our comfort zone. You can choose to
despise or embrace the process.

—••● ●••—

FOCUS ON YOUR GOALS

Remember, your goals are your target, your X on your map,
your bullseye.

It's imperative to keep your focus on your goals every single
day, multiple times a day if necessary. Before beginning your
day, each day, look at your goals. Visualize what it looks like
to go after those goals that day. What would be the needle-
movers, the steps, and actions that would move you towards
that goal?

Making your goals your focus helps you redirect yourself
when you are becoming distracted, directed, or reactive to
what is going on around you. It happens, and it's normal. But,
without clear goals being our focus, that's how we will end
up living life in reaction to all of those distractions and to
what's happening to us. When we are consistently focusing

on our goals, even when we have been slightly knocked off our path (or maybe even majorly knocked off, which again happens), we can look at our goal and make the necessary adjustments to get back on the path.

When you know where you are going, this helps you recognize what you are going to say "yes" to and, just as importantly, what you're saying "no" to. If you don't know what you're saying yes to, you will end up saying yes to everything that comes your way. You will be carried away by everything and everyone that is coming at you. You're yes is only as meaningful as your no.

Here's an analogy of keeping your focus on your goal, which came out of a real-life experience I had last summer in Puerto Rico.

My sister-in-law asked me to join her, my niece, and my nephew on a trip to Puerto Rico and plan that trip since they had never been to the island. We booked the trip and had a great week in Condado, the area of San Juan I used to live in, which was two blocks from the beach.

One day, we went to the beach I used to go to every day when living there. I let my sister-n-law bask in the Caribbean sun with her cold craft beer and enjoy some time for herself. I told her I would go with the kids to swim in the ocean and keep an eye on them.

The kids and I got into the water, and the waves were powerful and showing off that day. At this time, my niece and nephew were 10 and 14 years old and were not the strongest of swimmers; to say I was paranoid would be an understatement! I watched those two like a hawk! After being in the water for 20-minutes or so (my full attention on them that entire time), I took a second and looked up at the beach and didn't see my sister-n-law anywhere. I continued scanning everyone on the beach and didn't see her. I began thinking, maybe she left? Then my mind went to, "I said I'd give her a break, maybe she left me with the kids?". I had all of this confused inner dialogue going on while searching the beach.

I took my gaze from looking straight at the beach to looking up to the buildings that were around us. You see, this was the beach I would swim in several times a week when living in Puerto Rico, so I knew this beach well. I then realized the buildings that were in our proximity were not the buildings I was familiar with.

Since my focus had been 100% on the kids and not once glancing at the beach, I had become unaware of the fact that the waves had taken us several hundred feet from where we had first entered into the water and where my sister-in-law was set-up on the beach.

The keyword there is: unaware.

When you aren't living life in self-awareness and focusing on your goals, you will be carried away with life's waves. You end up wondering where you are and how did you get here?

Each day has an invitation and the opportunity to practice self-awareness, evaluate where you are, and decide where you want to go. Once I realized all of my focus had been on my niece and nephew, which allowed the waves to take us down from our location on the beach, we worked our way back that way; simultaneously, I was keeping an eye on my niece and nephew.

When you have a goal, you can navigate your way back towards your goal when life happens. You can make the adjustments, corrections, and actions necessary to correct your navigation. This is both done in the mental and physical.

Read over this chapter a few times, take notes, write down your ah-ha moments. Write down your S.M.A.R.T. goals. Create goals from your wheel of life.

Do the work. Be committed to yourself, your goals, and the adventure. Don't be surprised if, along the way, you give others permission to do the same as they watch you transform.

Ah-ha's and Discovery

How did you feel about goal setting before beginning this chapter?

_____

_____

_____

How do you feel about goal setting now?

_____

_____

_____

What have been some of your biggest challenges in setting goals in the past?

_____

_____

_____

How do you want to show up now with setting your goals?

_____

_____

_____

And... ACTION!

Write down at least two challenging goals using the S.M.A.R.T. method. Visit your wheel of life to decide what your goals are going to be. Write down goals for the other areas as well that you want to work on this quarter actively.

Look at your goals daily. Look at them (at minimum) in the morning and visualize what it would look like to reach your goal. Plan your day around your goals. Look at them however many times a day that helps you focus and remain motivated.

Needle-movers: What would be the daily, weekly, and monthly needle movers for your   goals? The steps and actions that would make significant progress towards your goals   becoming your reality?

Who do you need to recruit to help you with your goal(s)? Write down a list of people or what kind of expert/coach you need to find to help you reach your goal and reach them FASTER.

Adventure Roadblocks: Limiting Beliefs

---◆━---

"You don't become what you want, you become what you believe." -Oprah Winfrey

---••●••---

G et comfortable. We are going to be in this chapter for a while. This is probably the most critical chapter of this book. We are going to discuss, expose and find out how to transform limiting beliefs.

I used to have no clue what limiting beliefs were. Like most people, I was unaware of what was unconsciously driving my behavior. My limiting beliefs continually sabotaged any progress in my life and caused me to dream small, if it all. They were what was at the root of why I would stop moving forward whenever an obstacle came my way.

Whenever I am asked to speak or teach, limiting beliefs is always included in some part of what I share. This is because it is so important to understand them. As they are 99.9% of the reason, we don't accomplish what we set out to do or live the life we desire and why we fail to become the best versions of ourselves.

WHAT ARE LIMITING BELIEFS?

Research has shown that most of our values (the things we believe are important in the way you live and work) and beliefs (an idea that we hold to as true) are established within us by the age of six. Yes, six years old.

That is because up until that age, we are little sponges; we absorb and believe pretty much everything that we learn, hear, observe, and experience from our caregivers. Think about it, most of us believed in Santa Claus, magic, the Tooth Fairy, the characters, and what they were capable of in the books we read and the movies we watched. That same childlike belief and wonder were also applied to us, believing anything our parents or caregivers told us or we experienced with them and through them.

Research also shows that at least 80% of the beliefs we adopt are internalized as negative. This can be attributed to several things. One can be due to the experiences being negative, and the other is that it is our innate human nature to gravitate towards the negative.

With bringing attention to the negative experiences we may have encountered as children, this isn't intended to be an opportunity to bash our parents or caregivers. Most parents and caregivers do not have the agenda to deposit negative values and beliefs, and most parents are trying to do their very best they can.

Even with the healthiest of households, parents, and caregivers, nurturing, that number still holds. So, this isn't an excuse or opportunity to go after or blame your parents and those who raised you. Again, they were trying to do the best they could with what they knew. It's to have an understanding. They are parenting through their own childhood experiences and deeply deposited values and beliefs. I will say that not all beliefs are limiting, and not all limiting beliefs are horrible or stem from some negative experience. They are just that, limiting. Some may have been beneficial or needed for a specific time in our lives, but now, they are no longer required and can be hindering our progress.

Our limiting beliefs are stored up in our subconscious, which makes them sneaky. Our subconscious is a lot like a tape recorder and will play the same behavioral responses to life's signals over and over again, usually to our destruction. This will continue to be the case if we don't begin to practice self-awareness and catch ourselves in the act.

You see, you can't change anything that you are not aware of, and in this case, we are talking about a limiting belief system.

WAYS THAT LIMITING BELIEFS ARE DEPOSITED

I will start with the root of limiting beliefs and work our way from there because it's so important to get this. Limiting beliefs are what keep us from living the life we are created to (limiting beliefs about God, ourselves, people, possibilities, life, etc.). The flip side is that when we can transform our limiting beliefs (renew our minds), we can become, achieve, and make the life we were created to live *a reality*.

> *You see, you can't change anything that you are not aware of, and in this case, we are talking about a limiting belief system.*

---·•●●•·---

As mentioned, most of our values and beliefs were deposited into us from birth until the age of about six years old and come from experiential memories downloaded into the subconscious mind.

They were deposited into us by:

1. Parents/caregivers

2. Mentors, teachers, extended family members, babysitters, religious trainers, etc.

3. Traumas

Again, the research concluded that at minimum, 80% of our internalized beliefs have a negative orientation, and that's if you were raised in a healthy home or environment, which isn't the case for most of us. Think about it. What's the first word we usually learn as children? That's right. "No."

There are beliefs that we learn as children that are necessary for our safety, but as adults, they no longer serve us. For example: "Don't talk to strangers." As children, that is important. There are a lot of crazy people out there! But as an adult, if we continue to carry that belief, then we may be limiting ourselves in meeting new people, which can also impact connection, overall happiness, and achieving our goals.

COMPASSION AND CURIOSITY

You may experience being uncomfortable when first beginning to identify your limiting beliefs. Again, that can be attached to a belief that you are flawed in some way or something is wrong with you. If you find yourself attaching judgment or shame to the exposed beliefs, catch yourself when doing so.

I am not sure what or who you believe in, but I will share a core truth that I live by. I believe in God, but whatever you believe in, insert it here. I learned that God does not reveal anything (including our limiting beliefs) to shame, condemn, or judge us. His intention when revealing anything is always to lead us to healing, deliverance, or to educate us (by renewing our minds).

When digging into your limiting beliefs, remember to utilize the essential tools you packed as you began this journey and treat yourself with compassion and curiosity, like you are dealing with a dear friend. Treating yourself with compassion and curiosity is crucial to personal development and transformation...and living your adventurist life.

Limiting beliefs are like layers of an onion; there are many layers to your belief system. Don't try to go in and reveal everything at one time. You have a lifetime for that, and it would be completely overwhelming if you did. Take each belief as it comes and process it.

Once you begin to identify them, it can become addicting, as you find yourself saying, "oh, that's why I do that or think that way!" and then you get to transform the belief (renew your mind). You realize the power given to you to change your mind!

HOW TO BEGIN UNCOVERING LIMITING BELIEFS

This is where the fun begins. Okay, it may not be fun at first. Trust me; you will come to enjoy this part of the process once you are committed to taking the actions and seeing the results and transformation in your life. Let's dive into some steps and tools to begin uncovering your limiting beliefs. Remember, our limiting beliefs are played out in our behaviors, more specifically, revealed in our patterns.

Our patterns reveal so much about our beliefs (beneficial ones and limiting ones). We can't fake our patterns. They are driven by our subconscious and will come to the surface one way or another. Begin thinking about any pattern or patterns that you can identify in your life. It can help assess the different areas and situations (referring back to the wheel of life) and begin recognizing constant obstacles you experience, your patterns of behaviors, and thoughts that conflict with what you consciously want to happen in your life.

Limiting beliefs are like layers of an onion; there are many layers to your belief system.

———————•••●•••———————

Here are some areas of life and topics that you can begin thinking of the patterns you see played out in your life:

Romantic relationships

Friendships

Communication

Intimacy

Parenting

Health & Wellness

Relationship with food

Physical activity

Career

Education

Conflict

Self-talk

Money

Identity

How you view yourself

Spirituality

How you view God

You are not limited to those topics and questions, but they will hopefully get you started with uncovering your limiting beliefs.

After doing years of research, Amanda Goldston, author of Clear Limiting Beliefs, concluded that there are Top 10 Limiting Beliefs, and they are as follows:

1.The Fear of *Greatness.*

What if I was great at my own business? My job? As a spouse/partner? As a parent? A public speaker? Author? Athlete? Etc.

What would other people say? What would my family and friends say if I were to outshine them suddenly? What if my income took off? I bought my dream home or my dream car, etc.? Interestingly, for most people, this is one of the most uncomfortable thoughts they can consider, and that is what holds more people back more than anything else.

Does this go in line with the Our Deepest Fear quote from Marianne Williamson's book Return to Love mentioned in the introduction chapter? Yes, it most certainly does. Please take a moment and read that poem again.

How did you feel reading that poem? If you aren't feeling it yet, I encourage you to read it again and then again. Read it out loud with confidence in your voice. Read it while looking in a mirror. You can even try replacing the words to make it more personal and in the first person. This is yourself you are talking about. What does it look like for you to shine? What does it look like for you to be powerful beyond measure? For you to make manifest the glory of God?

I have this quote posted on my refrigerator, and it always gives me a shot of life when I read it. If you need to post it somewhere as a reminder, do it. Don't believe the limiting belief that playing small serves the world in any way. You are a child of God. Let that light shine!

2.The fear of *not being (good) enough.*

I am not smart enough, strong enough, thin enough, pretty enough, manly enough, liked enough, interesting enough…You fill in the blank:

I am not _____ enough.

The belief holds so many people back—the feeling as though they are not enough or good enough.

What if everything you need to succeed is already within you? Guess what, it is. It's just a matter of unlocking it and believing it. Imagine if you believed what was necessary to achieve your dreams, goals, purpose, to experience this life deeply?

Let's flip some of those common "enoughs" listed above….

I AM smart.

I AM strong.

I AM beautiful.

I AM manly.

I AM liked.

I AM interesting.

And so on. It changes everything. We will get into "I am" statements later as the tool that transforms our beliefs and renews our mind. But you're getting a little taste of it right now.

If you didn't already know, fellow adventurist, you are enough. You can become your fullest authentic self. You can unlock what's in you. You can live out the life you were created for. You can deeply experience this life. You just have to begin believing it.

3.The fear of *not being loved.*

The fear of not being loved is linked to the previous belief. People often believe that if they are their true selves, others will not love them, that they will lose those closest to them: family, friends, co-workers, etc.

Many people go through most of their lives trying to be what they think others want them to be, to be accepted and loved. This can keep us from fully living life, being our true selves, and feeling like something is missing. At our core, we all want to be known, accepted, and loved. When we try to be what we think others want us to be continually, it's a false sense of acceptance and love. This kind of behavior keeps us in a pattern that, in the end, leaves us feeling empty and unsatisfied with life.

First, you want to develop a strong sense of who you are, love who you are, and how God made you. Celebrate how uniquely you're made and get to know you. From that place, you can begin to invite others to experience the real you. If not being loved is one of your limiting beliefs, you can create an "I am" statement to begin transforming that belief and renewing your mind. Example: I am loved. Don't worry; we will get into this more later in this chapter.

4.The fear of *rejection.*

This was a limiting belief for me. I would never "put myself out there" for fear of someone rejecting me (in dating, friendships, my input in social and work settings, etc.). I would often reject someone else, a situation or opportunity before they had the chance to reject me. I always envisioned the worst-case scenario.

This behavior kept me from offering up ideas. It kept me from sharing what few dreams and aspirations I had. It kept me walled up, and I wouldn't allow anyone in. This fear of rejection can show up in many ways, from not asking someone for a date to not ever presenting a business idea, or pursuing a business venture, or not making that important call, or having that difficult or much-needed conversation, you get the idea.

What if the person or people on the other side say "no"? No is the word we fear, that if we get a "no," we are being rejected as a person, instead of seeing it as they are rejecting the offer, not you as an individual. What if the worst-case scenario was that they did say "no"? You can chalk it up as a learning experience, as all things are if we allow them to be.

What if they said yes? You're never going to experience the "yeses" without putting yourself out there and experience some no's. Life is too short and too precious to play it safe by never putting yourself out there. Success is a matter of asking and keeping on asking. Success is a matter of being brave enough to put yourself out there and keep on putting yourself out there.

I mentioned before; when I was a child, I was very shut down. Most people did not know (and by people, I mean my dad, my mom, and my sister, as I did not have many friends) is that from as early as the age of seven, I would dance privately in the den of our home.

My music of choice? My favorite was Prince's Purple Rain album. My favorite song choices from that album? Let's Go Crazy and When the Doves Cry. Those two songs I would dance my little heart out to. Let's Go Crazy was for my crazy energetic side (which did not come out in its fullness until my mid-30's), and the song When the Doves Cry was for my more sensitive and interpretive side (I am somewhat joking as I share this, but there is some truth to it!). If you have a chance, listen to those songs, and you will get a mental picture of seven-year-old Felicia and the story I am sharing.

I did this for years, privately, secretly. I would have so much fear that someone would walk in one day and catch me dancing wildly. If I heard someone coming towards the door or coming into the house, I would hurry up, turn off the music and stop dancing. What was my fear? Embarrassment. That someone would walk in and laugh or look at me crazy. They would reject my dancing abilities. I never allowed anyone to catch me, nor did I ever share it with anyone.

I loved dancing and still do. It was an insight into my passions and desires. Flash forward now three decades, and I still love dancing, but it looks a lot different.

I have now been dancing salsa for over four years. I am no longer that little girl hiding, but it didn't come without the work to uncover that limiting belief and change it. Dancing salsa has helped to reveal additional layers to my limiting beliefs. Because with each new level we go to (including salsa dancing), our beliefs will be challenged.

How are things going now with dancing? Oh, now I'm that girl who has no problem dancing in front of a lot of people (actually give me an audience!), and since we are talking about the fear of rejection, I have no problem asking a professional dancer to dance! I seek them out! Did that happen overnight? Most certainly not. Has it been worth it working through the layers to become who I was created to be and be that girl that puts herself out there?... heck yes!

5. The fear of *failure*.

What this boils down to is: "what if I try this, and it doesn't work out?". Failure is often looked at as something that should be avoided at all costs. How many of us don't step out into life because of this fear?

Often, those that experience success in their lives and feel as though they are truly living life would say they have experienced many "failures" along the way. Instead of looking at them as failures, the only difference is that they look at them as learning opportunities.

As the quote by Wayne Gretzky goes: You miss 100% of the shots you don't take. Let that sink in. You can play it safe your entire life and end up at the end of your life with all of the regrets of how you wished you had shown up.

Those that come to the end of their lives feeling confident and satisfied with the life they lived are not those with regrets of "I should've tried or done _____." They, who chose to live bravely, are the ones that took the risks of deeply experiencing life and taking some shots. They took chances on relationships, ideas, experiences, opportunities, businesses and got out of their comfort zones. They chose to show up as themselves and invited others to do the same. They had ideas and acted on them. They set big scary goals and pursued them. They surrounded themselves with a community and sought out the support they needed, and they were there to support others. They embraced their unique life adventure and lived it.

You can play it safe your entire life and end up at the end of your life with all of the regrets of how you wished you had shown up.

---•••●•••---

Here are questions to ask yourself to help reveal what you want and move past the fear of failure:

"If I were informed that I only had three months to live, what things would I have regretted not doing? What would I say to those I love and the world? What would I make sure I would do before the end of those three months? What is the impact and legacy I want to leave?"

Your answers to these questions are very revealing. Take time to answer them as if your life depended on it.

I ask myself those questions often. Quite honestly, it now scares the crap out of me to waste the precious time I am given. When I ask myself those questions, it's what I need to put fuel and necessity and urgency to my actions, to where my daily actions reflect a life of having no regrets.

Decide you're going to take action towards what is awakened in you. Think about what you would do if you weren't afraid of failing?

There is something that happens when people are faced with the reality that the end of their life is drawing near, and it's called clarity. For some people, they were already living their life in a way where they had no regrets and can honestly say they lived life their life to its fullest. But, for other people, unfortunately, the majority, the clarity they receive is that they know immediately what is important to them, wishing they had more time to live truly, and are left with the feeling of so many things undone while on earth.

All of this isn't intended to bring doom and gloom, but a reality check that we all need and to reiterate that life is precious and frail. As a verse in the bible says, our lives are but a vapor. The truth is, all of our realities are the same. Tomorrow is not promised. You have to make the decision that you are going to live life every day as a gift. What would it look like for you to live every day as a gift?

A quote from the movie Shawshank Redemption that I love and hits me at my core is: "get busy living or get busy dying." I am guessing since you are reading this book, you want to get busy living. Make the decision that's exactly what you are going to do, get busy living!

6.The fear of *success*.

This one is similar to the fear of failure and the fear of greatness. This was one of my greatest limiting beliefs that was exposed in my later 30's. I will get to that story in a moment.

Change can be scary, and that includes positive changes. This is usually because somewhere deep down, we have a fear of success. What if I outshine those around me? What if those closest to me were to say, "who does he or she think he or she is?".

This can also be from past experiences that have reinforced this limiting belief. That was my story. I was a "runner" from success, as my mentor told me during our first counseling session. This is what happened that day my life changed.

As I mentioned in the introduction of this book, I was invited to a seminar on the D.I.S.C. personality styles, which was facilitated and taught by, who is now my mentor, and who God used to change my life, Dr. Allen McCray (who I call "Doc"). In all honesty, I was not very excited about attending this, but two dear friends of mine said I needed to go. Sidenote: make it a priority to get yourself a friend or friends that are consistently pushing you to grow.

So, I went to the seminar. And like I said, it was an all-day-long seminar that I wasn't too excited about attending but ended up being engrossed in every single second of this workshop. The 8-hour workshop felt more like 2 hours, and at the end, I was left wanting more. I still have my notes from that day. I had to find new places to take notes on the handout given because I was writing down everything single thing I was hearing. I felt something awakening, something shifting.

Until that moment, I knew there was something more, something that ached inside me that said there was more to life than I was living. Like a lot of us, I had no clue how to get it. This ache and desire had been going on for almost a decade.

A brief recap: after the seminar, I went home, was doing dishes, a flood of emotions hit, and I lost it at my kitchen sink. And let me stress, lost it, emotionally lost it.

Until this moment at the kitchen sink, I was the one who was intolerant and uncompassionate when it came to people who were not able to hold themselves together emotionally. This came from a childhood of emotional ups and downs with emotionally unstable caregivers. This had caused me to decide (unconsciously) that I would not be that way and always had to be a level-headed and emotionally together individual. I would keep everything together for myself and to be the stable one for everyone else. I could have been referred to a time or two as being an ice beast, true story.

All of this prompted my first request for counseling that was not court-appointed (yes, this girl does have a past). I sent an email to Dr. Allen McCray asking for a counseling appointment. I remember it like it was yesterday. I was waiting in his office waiting room. I was incredibly nervous, as though I was at a job interview for a job I wanted. I felt like I was going to throw up. In hindsight, I feel like my body and mind knew the significance of the God-ordained session I was about to walk into.

I walked into his office and sat down in one of the comfy chairs. I found it hard to look him in the eye. He had his legs crossed and had his arm rested on the arm of the chair while resting his head on his hand, as you would picture the idea of what a counselor would look like. The dialogue of our session went something like this:

Doc: "So, why are you here?".

Me (already crying): "I am here because of your seminar."

Doc (cracking a little smile): "why are you crying?"

Me (again): "because of your seminar."

Doc: "my workshop is not why you are crying. What is it that you are thinking about right now?"

And that's when it came to me.

Me: "the spelling bee I was in when I was eight years old."

There, I said it. I realized that was one of the memories that I had been brought to the surface during the seminar (along with many others). My self-awareness had been awakened that day, along with my emotions and quite a few buried painful memories.

I began sharing how the story of how I was an A+ student, on the honor, and I had a lot of expectations from my dad to over-excel and over-achieve. At the age of the memory, I am about to share; I was eight years old. I was continually tested for gifted programs and was an excellent student, and was extremely shy and introverted. When I was in third grade, I made my way to the intermediate elementary school spelling bee. I made it to the final four contestants and then the last two. It came down to a second-grade boy and me.

We dueled back and forth for what seemed like hours, an eternity to this eight-year-old little girl, for the title to be the Bloom Elementary Spelling Bee champion. I still remember the stress, thinking, "will this ever be over?" I also remember I had searched and zeroed in on where my parents were sitting in the auditorium. They were right off the middle aisle, at the end of a row, and about half-way between the front and the back of the auditorium.

Finally, let me stress, finally, during my participation in this torturous spelling bee battle, I was given the word "bye." I am not even sure if that is the correct word in its context now. I think I chose to block it out. But, as you know, there are several different ways to spell the word bye depending on the context by which it's used. There is bye, buy, and by. Whichever one it was (which they use in a sentence, so you know which one they are referring to), I spelled the wrong one, the agony had finally come to an end (I thought), and I was relieved and devastated at the same time.

I ran off the stage crying (yes, this really happened) and ran dramatically towards my parents. I think I was looking for consolation, maybe out of embarrassment and shame? Not exactly sure, but what happened next is the memory that came out during my counseling session.

I ran to my parents (my little 5-year-old sister was with them), and my mom embraced me and said, "good job, baby." But my dad was visibly upset with me. In the middle of the school auditorium, he began scolding me, saying how he couldn't believe I misspelled that word and reminded me that I knew that word. I felt his disappointment. I felt like a complete failure.

And at 8-years-old, I said to myself and made an agreement with myself, "I will never put myself in this kind of situation again." And I didn't. That is what was exposed during the session. Not so much of what happened with my dad, but that I had been running from and sabotaging success ever since. I would constantly excel at things (naturally). But once things got too big or there was more on the line than what I was comfortable with, I would make adjustments (not consciously) to take myself out of the running.

141

It was a fear of success.

As our session continued, I was first challenged to forgive my dad and let him off the hook. He was doing the best with what he knew at the moment, and actually, we ended up having a wonderful and loving relationship later on in life that made up for all the decades we weren't close. In my session, I was asked what would it look like to let my dad off the hook for that experience?

I figured out what that looked like, and I did it. I forgave my dad for that experience and knew he was doing the best he could with what he knew at the time.

Then, Doc said: "you're a runner. You've been running from success your whole life". The statement hit me as hard as when I naively allowed my 6'1" brother to practice his rugby tackling on me. It struck me as if I was being hit with a ton of bricks or had gotten the wind knocked out of me. It took me a minute or two to catch my breath and my bearings.

If you've had any type of counseling, you may be familiar with the exercise he encouraged me to do. He told me when I was ready to do the following:

Take 8-year-old Felicia and put her in a chair, and tell her what you would have told her in that moment.

When I got home that evening, I did the exercise given to me. I pulled out a chair and put little Felicia in it (gosh, she was cute, two small braids, and missing a front tooth). I looked her in her eyes, and the first thing I told her was that she did a great job. I told her how proud I was of her. That this was just the beginning of her adventures, that next time she would do even better. I told her I couldn't imagine how stressful that was and how well she handled it and that I had learned from her. I thought she was so strong to she keep going even when she felt like giving up. That there was nothing that she could not do and that this was just the beginning of opportunities on stage. That I was proud she was mine and that I loved her.

Doing that exercise changed my life. Not only did it transform an actual experience, to where what I told the little Felicia sitting in that chair became my reality, and I began living from that place. It allowed me also to realize that I was not limited to transforming this one belief and experience, but I could change and renew all of the limiting beliefs that were holding me back.

I was empowered. I was changed. And now, I have talked to thousands on too many stages to count, shared my story, and the tools that changed my life to audiences all around the world. That if I can do it, they can do it, all from transforming that belief of being a runner from success to being a runner to it.

I hope that if this is a limiting belief you have, my story helps unearth that within you and gives you the courage and excitement to change yours.

7.*I don't deserve/I am not worthy* of success.

Who decides who is worthy or not worthy of success? God's desire is for all of us to be successful and believe we are created for abundance.

What's the criteria for someone to be considered worthy of or deserving of success? Is it family background? Education? Age? Sex? Have you put those criteria on yourself and deemed yourself not worthy or undeserving of success?

You get to choose that you are deserving and worthy of success right now. Remember, limiting beliefs are sneaky and are deep down in your subconscious. In bringing up these top ten limiting beliefs, it is in the hopes that it will help begin bringing them to the surface. We will be doing some exercises later that will also help to uncover such beliefs.

8.Rich people are _____.

You have to fill in the blank with this one. If some of your thoughts are along the lines of rich people are all mean, selfish, arrogant, unspiritual crooks, cheaters, uncompassionate, etc., then these beliefs may hold you back from, or at least make it very difficult for you to obtain wealth.

If that's how you view rich people, then it's unlikely you would want to become one, right? Even if you say you want to become a rich person, you will continue to sabotage yourself on a subconscious level until you adopt the belief(s) required to obtain that goal and sustain it.

9.I have layers of deep-rooted beliefs that hold me back.

This is when you are aware of the deep-rooted limited beliefs that are negative and hold you back, and you continue to choose to keep them. They become your excuse for the life that you are living.

You have the power to change a limiting belief. You have the capacity and invitation at any moment to choose to renew your mind and create a new belief. Creating a new belief makes a new neuropathway in your brain. It creates a new road in YOUR BRAIN. Now, if that's not cool, I don't know what is.

The keyword mentioned before is the word choose. You have to decide if you're going to do the work to uncover your limiting beliefs and then do the work to change them. You can begin shifting your mindset to taking personal responsibility for your life and your thoughts. You can start to believe that you have the power to change your life.

You will begin seeing yourself and the world differently. You will begin showing up as yourself, the true you, and that my fellow adventurer, is extraordinary.

10.I have to work long and hard for my money.

Cue song: "She Works Hard For The Money" by Donna Summer. You may now have that song in your head all day long. You're welcome.

We have been programmed that we have to work long and hard for money. Don't get me wrong, a strong work ethic and mastery are necessary for success, and I believe for satisfaction in life. But what if we've made creating wealth and success harder than it is?

Yes, you want challenging goals, projects, and purpose that grow you. However, what if generating wealth wasn't working 60+ hours a week and at the expense of having no time for family, friends, enjoyment, freedom. What if it turned out to be easier and created the freedom to enjoy life and experience it on your terms? Genuinely successful people have adopted the mindset and realized that you don't necessarily have to work harder but smarter.

You have the power to change a limiting belief.
You have the capacity and invitation at any moment
to choose to renew your mind and create a new belief.

―――――・•● ● ●•・―――――

There you have it. The top ten limiting beliefs broken down a bit. As with all things within this book, the hope is that something was awakened or revealed in you while reading the list. When things are revealed or come to the surface, it's a good thing. Remember, you can't change anything you're not aware of.

Do you know the proverb "ignorance is bliss"? The truth is, ignorance can keep you stuck for a lifetime.

UNCOVERING LIMITING BELIEFS

Be assured, limiting beliefs are most certainly there, and they are hiding in your subconscious. Your beliefs (the beneficial ones and the limiting ones) are what drives your behavior.

Our beliefs reveal themselves a lot in our patterns, in our patterns of speech, our patterns of behavior, and the patterns of sabotage.

Can you identify some of your patterns? You may be able to identify some right off the bat, but more than likely, a majority will be revealed as you begin getting very intentional in how you want to show up in your life and pursue your goals.

If there is a goal or a target you've wanted to go after for quite some time and you have set goals and have either never reached it, or have obtained it, but weren't able to sustain it, then there may be a limiting belief hindering or sabotaging that goal.

Begin asking yourself questions. What do I believe about this? What do I believe about myself? Get curious with yourself.

We all have internal tapes and a dialogue with ourselves that are playing continually in our minds. It's catching ourselves in those patterns of thought, those beliefs in how we're talking to ourselves, that helps us begin uncovering and identifying limiting beliefs.

What is your self-talk? What are your patterns? What are your behaviors? Fill in the blanks of the following sentences to help guide you into uncovering your limiting beliefs. You may have more than one response for each one, and you can continue to use these questions throughout life. With each new level of life, a new layer of limiting beliefs will come to the surface.

"I don't have _____ because_____."

"I am not _____ enough."

"I can't _____ because _____."

Were you able to begin identifying some limiting beliefs? Remember, they are in layers, and don't feel as though you need to try to hit all of them head-on at once. That would be too much to process and would end up overwhelming you. Later on, you will decide which one(s) you want to focus on transforming that are important to you in your life right now.

Here is a limiting belief that that wasn't too long ago revealed to me in my later 30's and after I had already known about limiting beliefs and knew how to transform them. This is an

150

example of beliefs being in layers. At this time, I was able to finally able (more accurately, chose) to identify a constant negative pattern in my life, and it had to do with communication.

I used to own a boutique called the Happy Hippie Boutique (cool name, right?). It began as my own, and then I partnered with my best friend (she is more like a sister than a friend) to co-own the venture. Side note: consider and weigh the pros and cons of going into business with a friend or family member before doing it because it is hard! We had already been friends for ten years before going into business together, and it is only God and his grace that we are still friends after the experience.

Going into business with someone can be very revealing about that person and, more importantly, revealing about yourself. Unless you have common goals (which I didn't know this fundamental at the time) for the business, you will have conflict. Also, if you don't understand the different personality types and have two chiefs in charge wanting to run the show and have all the power, it is pretty much destined for failure. At best, it will be a miserable collaboration. I would like to say that she is still one of my best friends ahead of time, and we no longer own a boutique together, thank you, Jesus.

But, as with anything, all of life's challenges and experiences can be used to learn and grow and are opportunities if we choose to look at them that way. I have no regrets about having a boutique or co-owning it with my friend. And the one limiting belief that the whole endeavor helped reveal made the entire experience alone worth its weight in gold, which was my belief about communication.

My friend and I argued a lot. When I say a lot, I mean a majority of the time. They were real explosive arguments. I would consider them more like fights, and there were times they became physical. I would be completed filled with rage and frustration. To make the story even more interesting, we were also roommates. She saw the best and the worst of me. Those closest to us have the greatest insights into our patterns of behaviors, our true selves.

When we would argue, it would usually go something like this. We would disagree on something (from the schedule of who would be working the boutique, to purchases, to money, to boutique set-up, etc.), voices would begin to rise, and we both were dead set stubborn on the fact that we were right. The argument would continue to escalate until I would be the one that would eventually say "leave me alone," and I would go find some room with a door (and a lock) for retreat.

Always.

I would go in a room, I would close the door, I would lock it, and I would be in my little world. For me, once I walked into that room, everything on the outside faded away. I wasn't in there thinking about the argument or the fact that my best friend was at the door knocking and yelling, saying we needed to talk about what we disagreed about. I would block everything else out as though it wasn't even happening. This happened for years. At least a decade of it was played out with my friend.

Then, five years ago, after I had already been in my growth journey for three years and working alongside my mentor in the personal growth field (sometimes we think we have arrived, but it's a continual process), the time had finally come where I chose to recognize this pattern of behavior and get curious with it.

My friend helped reveal this by something she said during an argument. By the time this happened, we were no longer business partners but still roommates, and we were in a full-on heated argument. You guessed it. I did what I always ended up doing. I went into my bedroom, shut the door, and locked it.

Outside the door, she was yelling, "you always do this." And at that moment, I had an "ah-ha" moment. A pattern was being highlighted, and it was not a healthy one. That day I got curious about why did I always do this?

And then it came to me.

When I was a child, my parents (who ended up getting divorced when I was eleven years old) argued and fought what seemed like every day and seemed even more explosive at night. And it would get physical.

I am two years older than my little sister and always felt like I needed to be her protector. When my parents began to fight, I would always get her and take her into the room that we shared, shut the door, and locked it. It was in that locked bedroom that I felt she and I were safe. We could lock out what was going on outside of that door and live in our own little world.

I dug deeper. The bottom line was as I had never been taught or seen healthy communication. My parents didn't know it for themselves, so they could not model it for my sister and me. My childhood communication experiences (which is how our beliefs are deposited) had taught me an unhealthy and ineffective way of communicating. The belief that I had adopted was that if you disagree, you can't talk it out. If you don't remove yourself from the situation, it will always escalate to being physical.

That day, I discovered where that limiting belief was coming from, and it changed the way I communicate forever. I created an "I am statement" (we are going to cover that next) for communication, and it was "I am a healthy communicator."

I visualized what me showing up as a healthy communicator looked like, sounded like, felt like, tasted like, and smelled like. Was it uncomfortable at first? Yes, because I had been running to rooms and locking doors for my entire life. This was all new to me, but little by little, I became the healthy communicator I wanted to be and visualized. I created that new neuropathway, a new belief. I have not retreated to a room and closed the door since that day. But I would never have been able to change that belief without becoming aware of it.

If we begin to get real and curious with ourselves, with our behaviors and patterns, we can start uncovering beliefs that hold us back. We can gain insight into what's been keeping us stuck in behaviors and the choices that hold us back from who we want to become and what we want to achieve.

RENEWING THE MIND WITH "I AM" STATEMENTS

We are finally to my favorite part! We had to lay the foundation, and now we will begin doing the work of creating new beliefs. You are going to learn how to create your I am statements! You've probably already heard of affirmations. I am statements are affirmations on steroids, and they work!

This practice changed my life, broke through the ceilings of the limitations I had put on myself, and has brought me to a new level after new level, time and time again. I do this practice every morning and when needed during the day.

The term "I am" statements was inspired from the bible verse: "Let the weak say I am strong" (Joel 3:10). It says, "let the weak say I AM strong." Make note, it doesn't say let the weak say I am going to be strong, I hope to be strong, or I want to be strong. No, it says to let the weak say I am strong. It is stated in the present tense.

You can create I am statements for yourself that help transform a limiting belief to create a new belief. This is how you do it.

157

First, you identify what is the limiting belief I want to transform? An example can be if a limiting belief is that "I am not enough." The I am statement you could create might be "I am enough." Typically, when it comes to affirmations, we are told to repeat our affirmations over and over. Sure, it's good to repeat positive affirmations, but this doesn't necessarily get it into our subconscious. This is because you aren't experiencing what you are saying. But, when you attach your five senses to the, I am statements, that is where you begin putting yourself in the future, and you start experiencing your I am statement in the present. It goes from head knowledge to heart knowledge.

It's through our five senses that our beliefs were internalized in the first place. Again, that goes for the good ones and the negative ones (which can also be beliefs that no longer serve us). You can think back on an amazing moment you experienced and relive it. What it felt like, sounded like, smelled like, tasted like, and looked like. The same goes for a traumatic experience or a negative experience. You can relive it all over again and again, as though it just happened yesterday.

To illustrate this even further. Which is the most celebrated holiday for the majority of people? Christmas, right? Why? Because that time of the year plays on all of our five senses so dramatically and powerfully. During that time, there are sounds we only hear at Christmas: Christmas songs, caroling, etc. We experience potent smells: baking cookies and pies and the aroma filling the house, Christmas dinner, and the pine smell of the Christmas tree. The tastes that we experience: again cookies, pies, Christmas dinner, eggnog, peppermint, etc. What does it feel like? Usually there is a crispness in the air, or on a more internal feeling, there can be a warmth inside our hearts, a joyous feeling inside our bellies with time with family and friends, listening to Christmas songs. And then, last but not least, what does it look like? The Christmas lights, candles, decorations, Christmas trees in their splendor, Christmas sweaters, beautifully wrapped gifts, you get it.

Did you just relive Christmas? That's because it's powerful when our five senses are attached to an experience. And that is why we connect our senses to our I am statements.

Going back to the example of "I am enough." If this were your I am statement, what would your experience be with that statement with your five senses attached?

What does it look like to be "I am enough"? What are you doing? What are you wearing? How are your mannerisms? How are you showing up? Is your head held high? Are you looking people in the eye? These are just examples for you to get the idea. But, with any I am statement, it's vital for it to include what each sense is for you.

What does it look like to be "I am enough"?

What does it feel like to be "I am enough"?

What does it sound like to be "I am enough"?

What does it taste like to be "I am enough"?

What does it smell like to be "I am enough"?

This is where your imagination comes into play. You are bringing the future into your present. I love how my mentor puts it, "an I am statement is a declaration of a future state of being despite the current reality."

With this practice, it's not a "check off my to-do list" kind of approach. You want to sit with it and give your full self into attaching your five senses. This doesn't take long (especially after you have been doing it a while), but the importance is the intention and remaining present while doing it. And it will be a life-long continual process.

Recognize and appreciate that this is a lifetime journey. That's what makes life so exciting, fresh, and new. That's what makes it adventurist living. We get the invitation to grow every day. There is always an opportunity for growth until the day we leave this earth.

It's not so much about the importance of arriving but embracing the exploration in your adventurous life. Continue to celebrate every win, every step forward, every goal reached, every new way you become more of the best you.

You may come to find that the successes and invigoration of going further than you ever have before (in all areas of life) becomes addictive.

With your I am statements, they all don't have to be so serious! They are yours! You get to create the ones you are going after, the things you want to achieve in this season of your life, and who you want to become!

Here are some more examples of I am statements that I have heard from people:

I am confident. I am a successful business owner. I am an author. I am loved. I am healthy. I am fit. I am open to a relationship. I am a loving wife. I am a fun mom. I am a world traveler. I am wealthy. I am an influencer. I make an impact. I am vibrant, etc. Your I am statements can focus on internal goals and outward goals. There is no limit to them.

An important thing to keep in mind when creating your I am statement is always to make it a positive statement and do not use negative language. An example of negative language would be: "I do not eat unhealthily." When we attach a negative to the statement, it anchors that belief even deeper and stronger. You want to change that statement to make it positive. The revised example would be "I eat whole foods," "I eat for fuel for my body," etc. It's like anything, where our focus goes; that is where our mind and actions go. Instead of focusing on what you don't want to do or happen, begin focusing on what you do want to do and happen.

I am statements have now become an essential daily practice in my life for the past six years and has been key, key, KEY to achieving the goals I have, dreams and ideas birthed, and the person I have become and continue to become. I will keep repeating this since it's worth repeating. There are layers to our limiting beliefs, just like an onion. With each new level of life, each new challenging goal comes with it the revealing of another layer of limiting beliefs. A new version of you is required for every new level.

> *An important thing to keep in mind when creating your I am statement is always to make it a positive statement and do not use negative language.*

When crafting your I am statement, think, "who do I need to become to accomplish this" or "what would I need to believe"?

One of my I am statements used to be, "I am the girl that every guy wants to dance salsa with." Notice, I didn't say I am the only girl, but I am the girl (I'm not selfish – wink). This I am statement impacted the whole way that I show up to go dancing. Remember, they don't need to be super serious! They can be fun!

What did it look like to be the girl every guy wanted to dance with? It looked like me walking in confident, yet approachable and playful. I made eye contact and smiled. I would stand with one hand on my hip. It sounded like salsa music and fast Cuban salsa (fast salsa is my absolute favorite). It smelled like the humid Caribbean air (this statement was from when I was living in Puerto Rico). It tasted like sweat from dancing so much. It felt like electrical current running all through my body.

Guess what; I became the girl that every guy wants to dance with. Not because I was the most amazing dancer, but because I was fun. Most of the guys I danced with would tell me you have such great energy, and your smile is amazing! If you had told me I would have been salsa dancing, let alone being the one every guy wants to dance with five years ago, I would have told you that you were crazy! But now, here I am. And I am statements, and transforming my limiting beliefs is what got me here.

You can experience the same thing too. You can live out dreams and goals you haven't even yet imagined. I am statements will be a key tool to helping you live a life of continual growth and a dash of adventure every day if you choose to use them and do them.

Remember when we discussed imagination in the earlier chapters? I am statements tap into your imagination. You visualize who you want to become and what you want to happen and bring it into your present.

I mentioned this quote by Einstein in an earlier chapter, but it goes well here too, and repetition never hurts: "Imagination is everything. It is the preview of life's coming attractions."

WHEN TO DO YOUR I AM STATEMENTS

The best time to do your I am statements is in the morning before beginning your day and at night before going to sleep. If you're going to commit to doing them just once a day, then definitely do them in the morning.

Here's the thing about I am statements, they work if you use them, and they don't work if you don't use them. I know, super deep.

Doing them in the morning is very important. First, your focus in the morning determines your whole day. You get to choose how your day is going to look and set your intention for it. You want to begin making your I am statements practice a part of your morning routine.

Second, science has shown we have brand new brain cells available to us every morning that are just waiting to be recruited to the new belief system, the new neuropathways we are creating. But, if we don't take those new brain cells by the horns and say you're being funneled into my I am statements and the new beliefs I am creating, they end up joining in with our already existing beliefs. I don't know about you, but I want those new brain cells working for me!

You get to choose.

I would suggest doing your I am statements at night also. This is living intentional, as you are choosing to have the last thing that you focus on before going to bed is who you want to become. Of course, you are not limited to only saying them at these times. Say them as often as you feel needed and when presented with a situation in line with what your I am statement is about or for.

Example: One of my prior I am statements was, "I am an engaging speaker." Yes, I did this I am statement in the morning and night, but also within a half-hour of when I was getting up to speak. And it worked.

Have fun with it. Play around with when, and in what settings you want to do your I am statements. Make it a pleasurable experience for yourself. Realize you are changing your brain, your belief system, your life, and you!

REAL-LIFE APPLICATION

Before ending this chapter, I wanted to share a story about a young man that put into practice his I am statements, and he achieved what his goal was and more.

I am honored to go to Haiti every year to teach and speak on tools similar to what you are receiving in this book. It's arranged and facilitated by an incredible organization there called the Blessing Institute. In addition to going every year, we have partnered with the Blessing Institute to train and certify their leaders as Life Impact Transformational Coaches (my mentor's company and the company I am part of). I love it. It is part of my life's calling.

Back to the young man. I was in Haiti, doing a workshop for 120+ young adults on how to break through limiting beliefs and renew the mind. Near the end of the workshop, I wanted to show them in real life how to do the I am statement practice. I asked who had a goal they were wanting to achieve but having some resistance.

A ton of hands went up, and a young man in his early 20's was selected—his goal: to get accepted into the Haitian police academy. If you're not familiar with Haiti politics and those in authority, there is a lot of corruption and known for that corruption. This goes for a lot of the police officers as well.

So, the goal already had my interest and the interest of the other participants.

I had him come up to the stage and sit in a chair. I asked him to create an I am statement that was in line with his goal. When he thought about the big picture, his goal was beyond being accepted into the academy; it was to become a police officer. His I am statement was: "I am a Haitian police officer."

I had him close his eyes and say his statement, and we went onto attaching his five senses. What does it look like to be a police officer? He was a little nervous at first, and then he began getting into it. He replied, "I see myself with my uniform on, it's ironed, I am looking good! I am on the streets of Port-au-Prince with the people. I am talking with them. I am approachable, I have a huge smile on my face, and so do the people." As he began sharing this, his whole demeanor changed. He sat up straight in the chair and began carrying himself differently.

The next sense, I asked him what does it feel like? He said, "it feels warm inside my chest. I feel full in my heart. I feel the affection I have for my people. I feel the Haitian heat on my head. It feels good." His chest began to expand as he began to sit even more upright in his chair.

What does it sound like? "I hear horns honking, the commerce of Port-au-Prince, people bartering, people talking, a lot of the sounds of life happening, I hear the people talking with me and me talking with them."

What does it smell like? "It smells like the dirty streets of Port-au-Prince. It smells warm. I smell smoke and dust."

What does it taste like? "It tastes like the dust and smoke of the streets. I taste some sweat from me being out on the streets in the heat with my uniform on."

By the time he had gone through all of the five senses and attached them to his I am statement, he looked completely different. Sitting upright, proud, chest out, head up, and a huge smile on his face. It was so incredible to watch. Everyone present in the workshop was experiencing him differently, too!

Six months after that workshop, I got a message from my friend in Haiti that it is over the Blessing Institute. He wanted to share something extraordinary about that young man. He said, do you remember that young man from the workshop? I said, of course! He said, I just found out that he not only got accepted in the police academy, but he was hand-selected to represent the academy and the Port-au-Prince police department in a United Nations conference in Boston, Massachusetts! Not only did he bring his future to him and get accepted into the academy, but he also excelled. That same character of the police officer he wanted to become, that he had attached his five senses to and visualized, set him apart to where he experienced more than what he imagined in his I am statement.

This was going to be his first time traveling outside of Haiti too! Another goal and dream of his!

I hope this story gives you some fire. Regardless if you're in a third world country or in a country where we already have it so much easier than the rest of the world, I am statements work, and you can do them and experience becoming and reaching the goals you desire!

Ready to bring your future to you? To begin creating your I am statements for who you want to become and what you need to believe to achieve your goals and dreams?

Yeah, you're ready. Now it's time to create YOUR I am statements!

Ah-ha's and Discovery

What in this chapter impacted you the most?

Have you already began identifying some of your limiting beliefs? If so, what are they?

_____

_____

_____

What is a pattern or negative behavior that has been revealed?

_____

_____

_____

And... ACTION!

What is a goal or something you've wanted to achieve (can also be a characteristic you want to possess) that you have either not yet obtained or have achieved but sabotaged?

_____

_____

_____

What is an I am statement you can create for the above-said goal?

_____

_____

_____

What are 1-2 additional I am statements you want to create? Remember, these represent who you want to become. If you're already living it, then it's not necessary for an I am statement.

_____

_____

_____

Say your I am statements, ATTACHING YOUR FIVE SENSES (key!) every morning before beginning your day and in the evening before going to sleep. And more often during the day as you feel led.

But say them and attach your five senses! Remember, I am statements work if you use them and don't if you don't use them. It's that simple.

THE ADVENTURE ZONE:
DECISION MAKING

"It's in our decisions that our destiny is shaped." –
Tony Robbins

Beep! Beep! You are entering the adventure zone! In this chapter, I will talk about decision-making and what's at play when it comes to us making them and not making them. Indecision is itself a decision.

It's essential to understand the decision-making process because our decisions or choices shape our entire lives. It's your decisions that make your life what it is or what it isn't. Let that sink in for a moment. If you're not happy with your life, it's more than likely a result of your decisions. And decisions include how you respond to life since we can't control everything in our lives.

We've all been there, I know I have, stuck in life, knowing there was something more and wanting more, but my everyday decisions reflected my comfort zone I was subconsciously choosing to live. When we begin understanding our choices, and the beliefs that are driving them, we can start making the decisions that support who we want to become and where we want to go.

As you begin making decisions that support your goals, at first, you may feel uncertain, challenged, nervous, like all hell's breaking loose and more – that's normal. That's you stepping out of your comfort zone. It's called a comfort zone for a reason. It's comfortable. Normalize the feelings of being uncomfortable as you step out. It is part of the process.

Understanding where you are in the decision-making process will help you know where you are when presented with decisions, especially those in line with your goals and where you want to go. The following concept has been adapted from Bruce Whetten's book Yes, Yes, Hell No. The following illustration reflects the two lines we live in between: the ceiling and the floor. The space between the lines is our

177

comfort zone, and our comfort zone's space varies from person to person. For some, it's more extensive, and for others, it's smaller.

Here are the two lines we live in between:

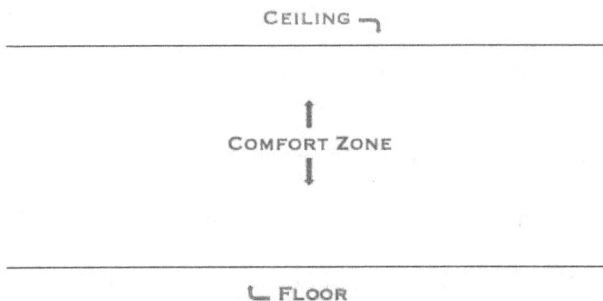

CEILING ⌐

‾‾‾‾‾‾‾‾‾‾‾‾‾‾‾‾‾‾‾‾‾‾‾‾‾‾‾‾‾‾‾‾‾‾‾‾‾

↑

COMFORT ZONE

↓

_____

└ FLOOR

COMFORT ZONE

The comfort zone is where pretty much everything is in automatic pilot and where we tend to make decisions on a subconscious level. No growth happens here. This is where a majority of people live their lives, in the comfort zone. The comfort zone can be broken down into every area of life: career, relationships, romance, health, wellness, money, fun, etc. Life here may come with having the feeling that life is "okay." Not great, but not bad either. Day after day can feel like you're living the same day over and over. But you know deep inside there is something more to life than what you are experiencing daily. Your decisions reflect life in your already established behaviors, habits, and thoughts.

THE FLOOR

Now, let's talk about the floor. The floor represents your bottom. When your life falls beneath your floor – this means this is as bad as you will let things get. An example can be in your finances. If your income or your savings fall below a certain amount, this is where an alarm sounds off, a "beep-beep-beep!" that screams danger, danger, danger, you've gone below your floor! I am not comfortable here! When this happens, you make the necessary decisions to bring your life back up into your comfort zone. When you've worked your way back up, then you breathe a sigh of relief, "ahhh, back in my comfort zone," and it goes back to status quo living.

THE CEILING

Let's get to the ceiling! Because it's when you begin to go beyond your ceiling where the real adventure and magic happens! The ceiling represents this is "as good" as you will let things get. This is reflected when you make decisions that take you out of your comfort zone in a good way. When you are experiencing something you never have before, it is here, when you are embarking on your ceiling, that a lot of limiting beliefs will be exposed.

In the same way that the "beep-beep-beep" sounded off when going below your floor, the same happens when hitting your ceiling. That's because your brain doesn't make the difference between good and bad. It just knows that something is different, that you are experiencing life different than when remaining in your comfort zone. The goal when making decisions is not only to get to your ceiling but to push beyond it. Here is where real growth happens, and your life's decisions begin to reflect who you want to become and where you want to go.

The idea is to continually be growing and raising the ceiling – to make that area where you live greater and broader.

Going further, there are three voices that control these two levels that we live our lives in between. In Bruce's book, he has classified the three voices as:

- the voice of *fear*, this voice *worries*

- the voice of *reason*, this voice *analyzes*

- the voice *intuition*, this voice *resonates*

The voice of intuition

This voice of intuition resides in our spirit, or some would prefer to say in their heart. It's trans-rational, which means that it goes beyond reason. It doesn't usually show up in our thoughts or ideas but *works more like a navigation system*. It clues us in on if we are on the right path or not.

This voice lights up around certain thoughts, ideas, and decisions. It resonates positively when we are on the course of our purpose, values, and beliefs. This voice also shows up when we "just know" something. It's trans-rational, where you can't fully explain it. You just know.

There may be many things that really don't matter to the voice of intuition. Whenever whatever is presented does not affect our beliefs, values, or purpose – the voice of intuition is silent. When we are on our purpose, the voice of intuition lights up. We feel a sense of congruency, joy, and inspiration.

In times of overstress, the voice of intuition speaks up, advocating for an increase of self-love or self-affirming choices. It lights up around the things that simplify our lives and that reduce stress and expectations. It's an advocate who supports self-care and slowing down. The voice of intuition is a big fan of breathing, stopping and smelling the roses, taking in each moment, seeing the beauty that is all around, enjoying life. It is our best guide to our highest good. It is always present but the most difficult to hear and the hardest to trust. Listening to the voice of intuition is something that must be cultivated.

The voice of reason

This voice comes from the mind and is not emotional. It is very pragmatic. The voice of reason's main objective is to be right. It analyzes the pros and cons and makes rational left-brain decisions based on facts and intelligence. Reason's job is to verify whether you're dealing with real and present danger, prioritizing your choices, and grounding your decisions. Its position is to help you move forward in the most efficient and effective way.

The voice of reason is great for creating and ordering priorities for steps to growth and success. It's good at figuring out what to say no to and when to say yes. We connect to the voice of reason by considering our highest values by sorting through relationships with win/win /win/ no deal criteria.

The voice of fear

The voice of fear comes from the body. Its basic emotions are fight, flight, or freeze.

This voice's job is to warn us of any danger. This voice comes before reason. It's important to understand that fear always reacts to change as scary. It doesn't know or care if the change is good or bad. It just recognizes that something is different, and so it interprets it as dangerous.

The voice of fear is here to serve you the best way it knows how. Its purpose isn't to stop you from moving forward (although that's what it can feel like). Its job is to warn you of potential dangers or change.

Great choices are inspiring, and yes, they are scary. When you make choices that line up with those big goals, those extravagant dreams, who you want to become deep within your heart, it will cause your intuition to light up brightly and your heart to sing. At the same time, those great choices will bring up your fears. And the bigger the opportunity, the bigger the step, the more significant the change, the louder and the trickier the voice of fear becomes.

The gift of everyday adventure, change, growth, and becoming comes when we begin to listen to our fears.

It sounds counterintuitive, I know, but it's true. We start with allowing the voice of fear to speak as itself, as fear, rather than pretending that it's the voice of truth. Change first begins to happen when we meet the voice of fear with acceptance and understanding.

When you do this and fear feels heard, it will release a lot of its energy. The voice of fear has something to tell you, and the thing is, it *wants* to be clear. It wants to let you know. And most of the time, when we listen with compassion, love, and curiosity, we can hear what it wants to say.

When we're facing real and present danger, all three of the voices will be in agreement. When there isn't a real and present danger, we need to ask what it is we're afraid of. That can be something new, something beyond our comfort zone, disapproval, lack of acceptance, failure, etc.

I am going to talk about the voice of fear a little more because if we are not aware that we are making our decisions in response to it, it can keep us from living life to our fullest, realizing our full potential, going after our dreams and goals and experiencing adventure in everyday life. The more we understand the voice of fear, recognize it and acknowledge it, the more we can learn to appreciate its place in our lives and that it's not out to get us. We can use it to bring more awareness and highlight our lives' areas that we may have limiting beliefs that are hindering us and our progress. The voice of fear is our friend. It means to help us, not to harm us.

The voice of fear speaks out of lack, scarcity, and loss. It screams out around decisions that would pull you out of your comfort zone. That is why so many people continue to remain in their comfort zones because they have been listening to the voice of fear.

Fears don't usually come in the front door and announce themselves by name. They are too sneaky for that. Instead, they typically show up in patterns. This voice shows up in negative feelings, insecurities, anger, frustration, worry, excuses, procrastination, and self-judgment. The purpose of the voice of fear is to avoid pain, guilt, shame, anger, hatred, and loneliness.

Fear isn't wrong, but it's addictive.

Our fears don't respond well to be told they're wrong. If you want the voice of fear to chill out, the first step is to listen to it from a place of love and acceptance. Then take action to move from through them to a place of courage, strength, and your adventure mindset. When you do this, you discover that love is more powerful than fear.

Often, as we move towards growth and things are improving, people will feel afraid that things are "too good," whether consciously or subconsciously. That is because the voice of fear is alarming that our decisions are taking us out of our comfort zone.

Remember, nothing great ever happens in our comfort zone. It's as we step out of our comfort zone that real growth, our potential, our adventure mindset, and living life to our fullest is experienced. Think about the voice of fear in the terms that it wants you to be and remain comfortable because it is a "safe" place.

It's called a comfort zone for a reason. It's
comfortable.
Normalize the feelings of being uncomfortable as you
step out.

———————•◦●◦•———————

When you can embrace the voice of fear instead of trying to fight it and genuinely listen to its warnings, a profound shift occurs. The voice of fear shifts from being an enemy to an ally. All of those unconscious thoughts and insecurities begin to fall away, and you can make the decisions that support the life you want, who you want to become, and your adventurist life where you are growing and evolving every day.

You will feel anxious and be uncomfortable as you begin making decisions that will take you out of your comfort zone. You can now identify when you're feeling this way and think about the ceiling and the floor illustration and realize you are hitting your ceiling and that you are about to move beyond it. The voice of fear would like to keep you in your comfort zone, again, not because it is terrible, but because it sees it as safe and anything else outside of it or different is dangerous.

When the voice of fear rises up, acknowledge it, thank it and then begin to try and understand it. Ask it some questions, like:

What are you trying to warn me about?

How are you trying to protect me?

What is the positive purpose?

In addition to safety, what are the positive outcomes or other goals you are trying to help me create?

I think about this illustration almost daily as I am continuously pursuing new goals and new levels. With each decision that takes me a step closer to my dreams and goals and is beyond anything I have ever done before, fear still sounds that alarm. Beep-beep-beep! It shows up a lot like anxiousness, and it also can be manifested in my procrastination if I catch it later rather than sooner.

> *You will feel anxious and be uncomfortable as you begin making decisions that will take you out of your comfort zone.*

―――――――――•◦● ● ◦•―――――――――

When I realize that its fear talking because my ceiling is being hit, I then get excited! I know I am making real moves towards living this life to its fullest and continuously unlocking a new layer of my potential. My usual go-to phrase for myself, which I say out loud when the voice of fear gets loud, is "Thanks, fear. I've got this! I *am* doing this!". Remember the limiting beliefs chapter and the importance of I am statements? It's in hitting my ceiling where many of those beliefs are exposed and how I decide what I am statements I will have for the current season I am in.

Can you see how important it is to know why we make the decisions we do? Our choices are what shape our entire lives. Let that sink in. If we genuinely want to live a life of growing every day in every area of life and profoundly experiencing this life, it will require making the decisions that pull us out of our comfort zone.

Yes, it will be uncomfortable.

Yes, life is worth it.

Yes, you can do it.

Do the work below for you. As you begin to identify the voices that are talking to you, you can start making the decisions that move you out of your comfort zone. That will push you past your ceiling, and you will find that your ceiling will get higher and higher as you go to level after new level.

And that is exciting! That is where adventure happens!

Ah-ha's and Discovery

What in this chapter impacted you the most?

_____

_____

_____

Have you already began identifying areas of your life where you are hitting your cciling and listening to the voice of fear? If yes, what are they?

_____

_____

_____

How does it make you feel to listen to the voice of fear instead of fighting it?

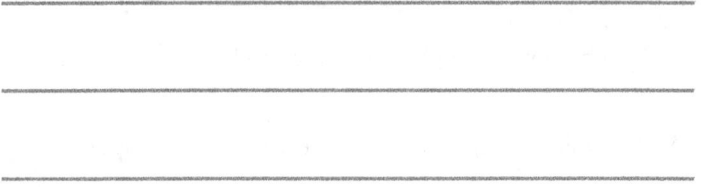

And... ACTION!

What will you do or say when you experience the voice of fear from now on? Write it below and say it this week when that occurs.

_____

_____

_____

What is an I am statement you can create for a ceiling or ceilings that you know you have been hitting?

_____

_____

_____

CREATING YOUR ADVENTURE STORY

———— ◆ ————

"If we own the story, we can write the ending." -
Brené Brown

———— ◆ ————

We learn through stories. Stories are how we understand and how we remember. Think about how we loved stories as children. I don't know about you, but I so looked forward to bedtime story time! Stories are powerful. With that said, we each have our own story with plots and storylines and ourselves as the main character.

We all have a narrative that is going on in our minds and hearts at all times. And, that inner narrative, our story, is what determines our life. We tell ourselves our story, and then our story tells us. It is manifested in our reality. Why is it that we resist change and resist changing a story that doesn't work?

Why do we as adults repeat the same behavior and patterns that don't work and often try to work them harder and expect a different result?

Part of it is our brain. Our brain loves repetition and patterns. That is because it is secure, it's safe (remember the voice of fear), and it is familiar. We repeat the same story because we know what the outcome will be. Have you ever witnessed a child (and adults do this too) that can watch the same movie a thousand times? That is because they find comfort in knowing the outcome, what comes next. It's safe and familiar.

With our stories, we are always loyal to the central theme and our lives' plot, continuing to return to it. When we enter into new territory (hello adventure) and begin developing a new story, it causes anxiety (hello ceiling) because we are experiencing something different than our comfort zone, other than the status quo. And since our brains and bodies like patterns and don't like anxiety, the easiest and fastest way to end that anxiety is to go back to the familiar: the old story.

There is always the pull of the old and the fear of the new. For life to change, for us to leave an old story, we need to have a new story to live from.

With new experiences, new neuropathways and new neural networks are formed. Through new experiences, through our new story, we create new highways in our brain. These then become our new neural pathways, and we no longer take the paths of our old story since we have a new one.

When we write a new story and change our minds, we are changing our brains. How cool is that? We can change our brains!

Here are some important keys to creating your new story, and this goes for every story of every area of your life. You have an overall story of your life (a central theme), and you also have a story you are telling yourself for each of the areas of your life: relationships, health, wealth, career, self-image, etc.

- **Recognize you are the author of your life.** No one can change your life or your story for you, it's yours, and it's your responsibility.

- **Own your present story**. All of your story is for your good and can be used for good. Instead of waiting for perfect conditions (which will keep you waiting forever), own the story you've been living, and then you can make the adjustments to change what you want.

- **Assess the storylines and plots.** What is the overall theme of your life story? Your adventurist living story? What are the plots that continue to play out? How do you, the main character, show up?

- **Decide what to keep, enhance, let go and avoid.** What parts of your story do you like and want to keep? What would you like to keep and take to another level? What do you know you need to let you go? And what is it you need to avoid to obtain the life you desire?

- **Author new experiences.** (This is where creating your new story comes from.) If life were on a scale of 1-10, what does your level 10 life look like? What I am statements would you want to create to begin living from that story? What do you need to visualize and start experiencing?

Most of the time, we focus on what is wrong with our lives, what we don't like, instead of focusing on what we do want in life, what we want our story to be. Remember, we get what we focus on, not on what we want.

In your story, what have you been telling yourself?

No one can change your life or your story for you, it's yours, and it's your responsibility.

————————•••●•••————————

Let's dive into owning your story more. Owning your story is also recognizing that your beliefs and your assumptions generate the possibilities you see. They are what end up dictating how you process and what you perceive. They are the lens through which you see life. You can see how limiting beliefs and the voices we listen to in decision-making can also help us uncover the beliefs and assumptions that would keep us in a story that is not serving where we want to go and who we want to become.

It is our beliefs that become our self-fulfilling prophecies because they create the story that we live out. This works both ways, both with empowering beliefs and limiting beliefs. I don't know about you, but I want to live out the empowering beliefs.

We have already gone through limiting beliefs in a previous chapter, but here are some examples of empowering beliefs:

- I will do what I decide

- I believe the decisions I make to be good

- I am competent to achieve my goals

- I can make money and be wealthy

- I can find a way to love my work

- I will teach people how to respond to me in a positive way by being positive

Here are some other examples of limiting beliefs:

- I'm not good enough

- I don't trust people to be supportive

- My opinion doesn't matter

- I don't have what it takes

- I will never make the money I need

- No matter how hard I try, I will fall short

- No matter what I do, I will end up suffering

As you transform limiting beliefs, you are creating your new adventurist life story. You can change your mind, and it will change your life.

Now, think about you living your everyday adventure story. Think about the life that you want. Pull from your wheel of life exercise you did. What does your fullest life look like when growing and becoming in all of those areas of life, living your level 10 life? This is how you can begin narrating your new story, your adventurist living story.

What are you doing? How are you feeling? What does living your perfect day look like? And who would you have to become to live out that story in reality? That is your story.

Write it down. Visualize it. Create the I am statements that support it, and watch as you begin living from that place! You are going to live your life of adventure! Feeling alive, learning, growing, and exploring new and unknown territory every day and in all areas of your life!

Ah-ha's and Discovery

What in this chapter impacted you the most?

What parts of your story do you want to keep?

_____

_____

_____

What new limiting beliefs were unearthed in this chapter?

_____

_____

_____

What does your new story look like?

_____

_____

_____

And... ACTION!

Write some new I am statements you have come up with as you're writing your new adventure story:

_____

_____

_____

Read your new story every day and visualize it.

Say your I am statements, ATTACHING YOUR FIVE SENSES (key!) in the morning before beginning your day and in the evening before going to sleep. And more often during the day as you feel necessary.

Design Your Days:
Developing Routines

———————◆━━━

"You will never change your life until you change something you do daily.
The secret of your success is found in your daily routine." –
John C. Maxwell

———————•◦●◦•———————

I don't believe in the concept of "time management." This is why: we can't control time and make it stop or do what we say. It keeps going regardless of what we do or what we don't do. Every day, for those that wake-up alive and breathing, we each are given the gift of 24-hours, 1,440 minutes, and 86400 seconds for that day. We can't manage time, but we can do, is manage and lead ourselves.

Our minutes make up our hours. Our hours make up our days. Days make our weeks, weeks make our months, months make our years. Our years make our decades, and our decades make our lives. Each day is a gift to choose what we will do with it. At the end of life, it will be what we did with these days that will have us satisfied in the way we lived or experiencing a sea of regret wishing we had more time to spend wisely.

Adventurist living is a lifestyle. Brendon Burchard's take on lifestyle is my favorite. It's this: "lifestyle is our daily reality of action." The lifestyle you are living and experiencing is 100% reflective of what you do daily. It's that simple. And it's oh so important.

I believe living an adventurist life, growing, learning, and exploring new territory every day and deeply experiencing this life begins with a reverence for life, which comes down to having a reverence for how we spend our time.

I used to live each day without purpose. Sure, I had a routine, but it wasn't one that served my personal growth or my dreams or goals (I didn't have any goals at the time). This is what my typical morning routine would look like: I would get up (late), rush to get ready for work, grab something quick to eat for breakfast, speed to work to make it on time, clock in, and spend 8-hours doing work that wasn't my life's passion (but I believe we can use all things to grow us), eat lunch somewhere in there (fast food or something unhealthy I had brought from home), eagerly look forward to clocking out (counting down the minutes and hours) and heading home, where I would watch endless amounts of television shows, eat dinner, occasionally hang out with friends, go to sleep and wake up and do it all – over – again.

The lifestyle you are living and experiencing is 100% reflective of what you do daily.

───────── ••●●●•• ─────────

If our lifestyle, our life, is determined by our daily actions – then it is important to design our day to support what will have us make the most of our time, be productive (not the same as busy) and make the moves towards our goals and dreams we have for all the areas of our life. When we design our day, we become intentional. That intentionality is reflected in the routines, the rituals, and the disciplines that daily keep us in the flow and congruent with where we want to go and who we want to become.

I will cover the importance of a morning routine, an evening routine, and how you block your time during the day.

Morning Routines & Rituals

There is so much research to support that if we are deliberate about our mornings and dominate them, it impacts our entire day and our productivity, which makes perfect sense. What we choose to focus on in the morning will determine our focus for the day. A common habit that most successful people share is that they have a strong morning routine that they do consistently.

There are many great books about morning routines, one of my favorites is "The Miracle Morning" by Hal Elrod. He covers in-depth the power of mornings and also the following acronym for what to include in your mornings: S.A.V.E.R.S., and this is what it stands for:

S. – Silence (can be meditation, just silence, for me, it's prayer and silence)

A. – Affirmations (I am statements, attached to your five senses)

V. – Visualization (picture you accomplishing the steps that will move you towards your goals and how you want to show up for the day)

E. – Exercise (get the heart pumping, your body is what takes you through this life)

R. – Reading

S. – Scribe (writing, journaling)

These are what he shares to include in your morning routine. You can allot as much or as little time as you'd like for each area and when beginning, start with a smaller amount of time. The key is to begin.

I post a lot about my mornings and the power of mornings on my social media. Those closest to me know I don't play around when it comes to my morning routine. It doesn't matter if I am traveling or if all hell is breaking loose. I may stray away for a couple of days, but I always find my way back to it because of its effectiveness and how it brings peace, freedom, and direction to my life.

"I wish I could be a morning person, but I am not," "it's too hard to be a morning person," "I can't wake up in the morning," and so on. These are what friends, family, and those who follow me on social media tend to say in response to me being a fanatic about the importance of a morning routine. What their comments show is that they have a desire to be a morning person but don't believe that they can be one. I believe every person can be a morning person and dominate their days. Again, it a lot of the resistance can go back to the limiting beliefs chapter.

But a lot of it has to do with mindset too. If you in your language and self-talk you are already dreading the idea of waking up a little earlier the next morning, guess what, you're going to dread waking up. It's that simple. And the odds are that, more than likely, you won't do it or complain the whole time and decide you don't want to do it anymore.

But, if you decide the night before and say something to the effect of: "I am looking forward to my morning tomorrow and waking up" or "I am going to dominate and make the most of my morning tomorrow," you are already setting the foundation for you to succeed.

Like with anything, if you're not used to waking up earlier in the morning or implementing a routine, it will be uncomfortable at first. But, as you begin to do it more and more, it becomes a habit and a habit that supports the way of life that you want. You will begin to see the results in your life and a more positive attitude towards life.

With morning routines, find what works for you. The S.A.V.E.R.S. are a great place to start if you are starting from scratch. As you start implementing each of those at the beginning of your day, you will begin to experience your days differently. I would encourage you to experiment and read other material and find other successful people's morning routines to get ideas, what they do and when they do it.

We are all different. Therefore, our morning routines will look differently. When first beginning, I would suggest trying a routine for a couple of weeks. See what's working for you and what you would want to change or something new you want to implement. As for me, I have 10-minutes of worship and prayer time that begins my day. I then do my journaling, and I give that an entire 15-minutes. That's because I tend to have a ton of ideas and things going on in my head, so I have come to find out over a decade of having a morning ritual, I need more time journaling than maybe other people need. I also don't fit in my exercise time until after completing my morning routine and then two blocks of 50-minute work time focused on my creative work. I know that the first hours of the morning are where I am my freshest and most creative, so I work and create content during that timeframe.

Find what works for you and what doesn't work for you, experiment, have fun with it and enjoy it. Regardless of what you choose to include, I will say that you always want to include your I am statements and focusing on your goals in your morning ritual. This will help you continue to head in the right direction and make the decisions that support them. I look at my goals, my wheel of life, and say my I am statements every morning as part of my routine.

Right now, begin thinking about your mornings and how you can start making them magical, where you begin your day focusing on the life you want and what your day would look like to make it a reality. What time will you wake up? Where will your magic morning take place? What will make it the most enjoyable for you?

Evening Routine and Rituals

Sometimes our evenings get neglected. We're winding down and see evenings as an opportunity to "check out." Don't get me wrong, we all need to relax and decompress, but our evenings need some love, attention, and intention, too. Sleep is critical (that could be a whole other chapter in itself), and how we wind down in the evenings and what we do several hours before we go to sleep can impact our quality of sleep. A good practice that I have taken from Brendon Burchard is the 3-2-1 evening. It stands for 3 hours before going to sleep, no eating, 2 hours before going to sleep, no work, one hour before going to sleep no screen time. It's that easy. In addition to that practice, I also have a cup of chamomile tea. I prepare my coffee for the next morning (so I can have the most beautiful magical morning, and my coffee is a big part of that), I plan what my next day holds and already know what my main focus will be when I get to work and then I read. I think about what went well that day, what I am proud of, what I am grateful for, and areas I can work on moving forward.

What evening routine do you currently have? What would you like to implement? Just like morning rituals, experiment and see what works for you and what doesn't. Try things out for a while to see if they don't work for you or if it's just taking a moment to get your flow going. There is no right or wrong – it's what's right for you. We are all unique in this life of adventure, and you get to design your day the way that allows you to thrive.

Day Routine and Time Blocks

We've covered the beginning and end of our days, now let's hit the bulk of our days – the daytime and "work" hours.

How do you want your days to look? Where do you want to expend your energy? What will you be working on for your goals, and just as equally important, when are you going to work towards it? What actions and steps support your goals that will be reflected in your day? Remember that goes for all life areas: relationships, career, hobbies and fun, friendships, finances, education, spirituality, etc.

Let's say you work an 8-hour day. What times and days are you going to set aside for the plans and steps for your goals? An example can be family goals. You know you want to spend 6:00 p.m. - 7:00 p.m. as dedicated time giving your children full attention and doing an activity. Or an example for your financial goals could be scheduling Tuesdays and Thursdays from 7:00 p.m.-8:30 p.m. you will take that online course on finances. Maybe one of your goals is to write a book. What days and times are you going to commit to writing? On a daily or weekly basis? Possibly you are working on developing a business; again, what times and days are you going to commit to working on that goal?

Get it solidified and put it in your calendar. Solidified means it's solid. If it's in your calendar, you're going to do it, commit to a day and time and follow through. This will make all the difference in reaching your goals and also how fast you will reach them.

> *We are all unique in this life of adventure, and you get to design your day the way that allows you to thrive.*

––––––––••●●●••––––––––

For those who work from home or create their schedules, let me share about time-blocking like me. This has been a game-changer in my productivity, creativity, and avoiding burnout. This can also work for those of you with more than several hours each day outside of your regular workday to crush some of your goals.

The idea is that you spend 5-6 hours working on your most productive and creative work. This is what moves the needle in obtaining and reaching your goals. This is based on an 8-hour workday. It is taking 60-75% of your time working on the things that matter, that move you forward. The rest of the time is on admin and the day-to-day things that need to be addressed (emails, texts, phone calls, bills, etc.).

With time blocking, you want to work in 45-minute to 50-minute blocks in focused work and at the end of each time block, take a break. Get up and move and do something else for a quick break and then return to do another time block of focused work. When you do time blocking, set a timer! Set a timer to go off at the end of the time block, and no matter what you are doing, get up and change gears. Do some stretching, dance, get a drink, listen to some music, do some grounding, take a short walk, water some plants (oh, that's me), etc. The important thing is to take a mental break. For all of those obsessive people that get on a roll and have a hard time taking a break, make yourself do it.

In the end, you will have more creativity, have more energy, be more productive and avoid burnout. It will make it more enjoyable too!

What are you going to begin committing to in your day? Will you start implementing the time blocking method? How do you think that will impact your day? How do you think it will impact your results?

Decide you are responsible for designing your day and that you can live the day in intention and enjoy it! Only you can choose how you spend your time, so make the most of it! When faced with the end of your life (which we all will have to do at some point), how will you say you spent your time? Will you have regrets, or will you know you took each day and lived it on purpose? You can! Just begin and develop the habits as you go! But, the key is to BEGIN!

Ah-ha's and Discovery

What in this chapter impacted you the most?

_____

_____

_____

What do you want your morning routine to include? List the activities and practices (and the time you will do it) below:

_____

_____

_____

With your days, which days and times are you going to allot towards working on your goals and dreams?

_____

_____

_____

And... ACTION!

When are you going to begin implementing your morning routine? What will be your attitude (your I am statements/your language) towards your morning? What challenges do you anticipate, and how will you respond?

_____

_____

_____

When are you going to begin implementing your evening routine? What challenges do you anticipate, and how will you respond?

_____

_____

_____

Add the days and times to your calendar or planner when you are going to work on the items in line with your goals. How do you feel about committing to the days and times you have solidified in your calendar?

_____

_____

_____

If you're doing time-blocking, what activities are you going to do in between blocks? Remember to set your timer and adhere to it!

_____

_____

_____

GO LIVE YOUR ADVENTURE

"The only impossible journey is the one you never begin."
— Tony Robbins

Your adventure is calling out to you. It always has been. I hope that during this book, it has been awakened to a whole new dimension, and you've come to realize everyday adventure can be yours – if you choose it to be.

The fact that you completed the book is a good sign that you are ready to live your adventure! There will be bumps in the road, unfamiliar paths, and landmarks at times. That is all part of the process. The challenge is to look at all situations as opportunities for adventure. It will change the way you experience life.

This is what this whole book is about, to experience life fully. Your adventurist light will shine brightly to help light the path for others to see the possibilities of their own adventure and call the life out that is also calling out to them. If I failed to mention this earlier, your adventurist life was never just for yourself. It is for the world.

As you begin living your life fully, it becomes an ignitor to friends, family, colleagues, those you meet in passing – nothing shines more brightly than an authentic and fully lived life. Remember, at the beginning of this book, I mentioned I hadn't seen a fully lived life modeled for the first three decades of my life. But, when I did experience someone that had what I didn't even realize I was searching for, it became a powerful magnet that provoked me to believe that fully living life was available to me and challenged me to explore and take action to get it.

Imagine a world where we were all fully living? My goodness, how rich and impactful and glorious would it be? I believe we can. It begins with you, then you impact your circle, family, friends, workplace, and those you encounter, and they then do the same.

It is true, you cannot lead others where you have not gone before, so you must begin to live your adventurist life first.

————————•••●●••————————

Once you start, don't be surprised to see and hear how you influence those around you. Adventurist living is contagious.

You cannot lead others where you have not gone before, you must begin to live your adventurist life first.

I want to share something with you that my father wrote me that reflects me beginning to live adventure as a part of my everyday life. His words are especially sacred to me, as he passed on several years after writing this, and it is the fuel to my fire to continue. He wrote this in response to me asking him, "Papa, how do I bring value to your life?" which is part of a self-esteem-building activity we do in our self-leadership class. Here was his exact response, "you make my life a lot fuller by having someone I love, always there for me. I know

I can count on you. That's a huge plus at my age. You light up my days, whenever I see or talk to you. You give me courage to pursue my dreams, because you are. The best value is I know you love me with all your heart. Love you."

The redeemed relationship I had with my father later on in life resulted from me deciding to live life fully every day, pursue dreams and goals and explore new and unknown territory in his and my relationship. Your family and friends are watching you, more than you know. And each unique experience you encounter will not only change you but be a catalyst for those you are blessed within your life. We are all so much more connected than we realize, and we are meant to help, inspire, impact, challenge, and influence one another. That is what is life is all about.

Alright, you, adventurist, have been handed your map. You're ready to go. Begin, step into your new territory, your unique experiences, squeeze every ounce of life and growth out of each of your every single day.

And so, your adventure begins!

WITH GRATITUDE

The author would like to acknowledge the following sources for quoting their transformational works:

- Dr. Allen McCray, Life Impact LLC. Adapted from D.I.S.C.overing Your Personality DNA workshop
- George T. Doran, S.M.A.R.T. goals
- National Endowment for Financial Education (NEFE), Lottery winner and bankruptcy statistics
- Bruce Whetten, Yes, Yes, Hell No
- McCray, Who's Behind the Mask
- Life Impact LLC, Adapted from the Impact Shift self-leadership course
- David Krueger, M.D., Live a New Life Story
- Jim Collins, Good to Great
- BJ Fogg Ph.D., Tiny Habits, adapted from Thrive Global on Small Wins,
- https://thriveglobal.com/stories/how-to-celebrate-small-wins-reach-goal-new-habit-change/
- Paul J. Meyer, Success Motivation Institute Inc., Wheel of Life reference
- Marianne Williamson, A Return to Love